UnConvenience NoMo - Recollections
By
Lincoln T. Beauchamp, Jr.
'Chicago Beau'

With
J. LaBosse

Kansas City   Toronto

UnConvenience NoMo - Recollections
By Lincoln T. Beauchamp, Jr.
'Chicago Beau'
With J. LaBosse
Copyright 2021
ISBN: 978-0-944602-06-5

Foreword by Scott Cashman
L.T. Beauchamp Publishing
www.LTBeauchampPublishing.com
Email: booksbeauchamp@gmail.com

All rights reserved. No part of this publication may be reproduced, distributed, or trans-mitted in any form or by any means, including photocopying, recording, or other electronic or mechanical methods, without the prior written permission of the publisher, except in the case of brief quotations embodied in critical reviews and certain other non-commercial uses permitted by copyright law. For permission requests, write to the publisher, addressed "Attention: Permissions Coordinator," at the email address above.

Cover photo: by Dooney O'Neill Beauchamp taken at Quinta Luz Clara, Loulé, Portugal
Inside photos: Beauchamp family archives and
LT Beauchamp Publishing unless indicated otherwise.

Disclaimer: This book is a combination of facts about the life of Lincoln T Beauchamp, Jr., and certain embellishments. I have tried to recreate events, locales, and conversations from my memories of them. In order to maintain their anonymity in some instances I have changed the names of individuals and places, I may have changed some identifying characteristics and details such as physical properties, occupations, and places of residence. The reader should not consider this book anything other than a work of literature.
L.T.B.

Foreword
UnConvenience NoMo
November 29, 2021

In the aftermath of World War I, American artists, specifically African American artists, established themselves in Europe as an alternative to the repressive racism forced upon them in America. Beginning with Sidney Bechet and Josephine Baker, new possibilities arose for expatriates as new roots became possible. This significant part of American history played out over the remainder of the 20th Century but as the last few decades passed Lincoln Beauchamp aka Chicago Beau lived out another kind of experience. He experienced the American community in France but didn't stop there. Rather, he found his way around the world absorbing cultures that he must have only dreamed of as a child. As it turns out, he broadened the European experience with his time in Italy and Greece and into Africa. He's become important to the music scene in Iceland. He's also had the Canadian experience in Montreal and Toronto. He has family in Toronto, a daughter, granddaughter, and other relatives. This has created a kind of cross-border intercultural vibe that is ongoing. And he's continued with his American adventure in Chicago, California and now Kansas City.

As a cultural anthropologist, I often describe culture as the things that groups of people know and do. Different people know and do different things. Their cultures are wildly dissimilar. The truth is, it's not a simple matter to move from culture to culture but Beau has the instincts of an anthropologist. He understands cultural distinctions. He knows that a compliment in Paris can be an insult in Oakland. He knows that the values that define relationships are not the same everywhere. This, I think, at least partly explains his ability to survive and thrive as he moves around the world forging a lifestyle that adds new dimensions to being an American expatriate in Europe.

Beau's upbringing in Chicago was his first exposure to American cultures both mainstream and African American. That led him to a clear understanding of the racism in the U.S. It also prepared him for the differences he found in Europe. In some ways, Europe's racism is more complicated. Josephine Baker was celebrated as a dancer but was never allowed to transcend her role as an entertainer and be accepted into the inner circles of French social life . The art of Africans and African Americas was studied and appreciated even as the artists were subjected to some kind of exoticism. I remember that shortly after my arrival in Paris in 1997 I met a couple of teenagers who were fully conversant in the discography of *Pharoah Sanders.* Try finding any American teens with that knowledge. So, there is an appreciation of African American culture. And, certainly post-World War I stories about French citizens defending African American soldiers from the racist outbursts of white Americans in France are many . Yet Beau is no romantic. He describes the treatment of American musicians recording in Paris by record company executives who thought they could get away without paying per their contract. He also tells us about the "barrage of racist insults" spewed by British tourists in Nairobi. This kind of worldview can only be gained by the lived experiences of a man moving about the world and using his intelligence and education to interpret it. You are getting an important set of reflections that developed because of his keen self-awareness and sensitivity. Beau has highly developed listening skills that help him understand people and that paired with his masterful storytelling engage us through these pages.

Beau's career has strolled all over the map, much as his travels have. From music to the Commodity Futures Market, the photography business and publishing, all have combined to provide income when he needed it. It's extraordinary, when you think about it, how one comes to be successful in so many different fields. Being able to communicate with such divergent people, it is no wonder that he is an effective writer and teacher.

I met Beau backstage at the Chicago Jazz Festival in 2009 when I was visiting one of my mentors, Archie Shepp. Beau had a relationship with Shepp that went back to at least the summer of 1969 in Paris when they recorded Shepp's *Blasé* album. It was a time of great social unrest and a civil rights movement that was on both sides of the Atlantic in 1969. A few months later they recorded *Black Gipsy*. That album was supposed to be issued under the name of Chicago Beau, but the record company pulled it out from under him by putting Archie on the cover as the leader. There was no resentment toward each other by these artists but rather an awareness of dirty games that can be played by businesses even after contracts are signed. I was not expecting to meet Chicago Beau in that dressing room in Chicago, but I knew his work well after first hearing *Black Gipsy* on the Amherst College radio station back in the 1980s. From there I immersed myself into a Black Gipsy listening experience that spanned decades with that record.

While Beau started his recording career with Shepp,

he's gone on to make important recordings as a leader and with the *Art Ensemble of Chicago*, *Sunnyland Slim* and *Jimmy Dawkins.* His songwriting is grounded solidly in the blues, yet he is not afraid to bring his subject matter into the contemporary political realm in which he is an advocate for culture change.

Following that meeting with Shepp, I invited Beau to teach some writing courses at Harper College to capitalize on his experience as a writer, editor, and publisher. His stories in this area are as interesting as those that cover his career as a musician. In fact, his extensive travels inform what he publishes, most recently in his newest journal – *Spandana.*

The life of Chicago Beau is in these pages. His family, his loves, his music, his writing, and his understanding of the world are all there. How the Civil Rights Movement in the United States had an impact on the world is in these pages. How a man can be shaped by a culture even as he works to change it is in these pages too. However, perhaps the biggest lesson he leaves regards embracing change rather than fearing it. Wouldn't America be better off with more people like that? I'm happy to be able to collaborate with him at various times and whether you have the opportunity to know Beau or not, his life will enrich you.

References:
Rose, Phyllis. *Jazz Cleopatra: Josephine Baker in Her Time,* New York: Doubleday, 1989. 86

Stovall, Tyler. *Paris Noir: African Americans in the City of Light,* Boston: Houghton Mifflin Company, 1996
Stovall, Tyler. 1996.15,41,73.

Scott Cashman, Ph.D.
Harper College
Palatine, Illinois

L-R: Scott Cashman, Archie Shepp, Daryl Harris, Chicago Beau
Chicago Jazz Festival, 2009

Acknowledgements

Once again, I am extending my deepest appreciation to my lifelong friend, *Jacmel LaBosse*, for these years of working with me to bring forth my memoirs. Of course, our meetings have also been pleasurable beyond his and my recollections of places, people and events. We've had lavish dinners, listened to great music, and enjoyed the company of many friends who we've known through the years. Because of Covid-19, our most recent meetings were conducted via Zoom, and although not in person as in the past, we made the best of the situation. Many thanks to *MiZsa LaBosse* for helping us get through a few technical glitches, and for the translation of some of our conversations. And MiZsa, thanks for sharing beautiful vistas of Bora Bora, and the Pacific from your verdant terrace; and be assured that as soon as possible, I will be sipping champagne with you and Jacmel as we converse and inhale the ocean breeze.

Scott Cashman, thank you for writing the Forward to this work, and thanks for many years of friendship, encouragement and sharing your knowledge across the creative arts.

Dedication
To Family, Ancestors, Elders, Cosmics.

Invocation
Ibo ara ago o
Moyuba
Ibo ara ago o
Moyuba
Omo de ko ni
Ibo ara ago o
Moyuba
Fe Eleggua Eshu Iona

Greetings O people
I bow to you
Greetings O people
I bow to you
I have come today
Greetings O people I
bow to you
Eleggua Eshu
move out of the way

Proclamations
My Negritude is not a rock,
Its deafness hurled against the clamour of the day;
My Negritude is not a thing of dead water
on the dead eye of the earth;
My Negritude is neither a tower nor a cathedral;
It plunges into the red flesh of earth.
                              Aimé Césaire

'Where is the peace of Uhuru?
Where is the unity of Independence?
Must it not begin at home?'
                              Okot p'Bitek

Table of Contents

Foreward
i

Acknowledgements
vi

Dedication, Invocation, Proclamations
vii

21 February 2019
Raphael Hotel
Kansas City, Missouri
1

21 September 2019
Le Château Frontenac
Terrasse Dufferin
Québec City, Québec
45

Selected Photographs and Mementos
70

14 July 2021, Via Zoom
Time For A Change
97

29 July 2021, Via Zoom
Excerpts From Book 1, *Too Much UnConvenience*,
and Onward
138

I got the key to the highway
And I'm billed out and bound to go
I'm gonna leave here runnin
cause walkin is most too slow
      From, *Key to the Highway*
        by Big Bill Broonzy

With Beguine Beauchamp
Father and Daughter Dance 2018, Kansas City, Mo.

UnConvenience NoMo - Recollections
Lincoln T. 'Chicago Beau' Beauchamp
Conversations with Jacmel LaBosse

It's been three years since J. LaBosse and I met during the Reykjavik Blues Festival at Hotel Nordica in Reykjavik, Iceland, to finish my previous book of recollections, Too Much UnConvenience, that was published in April 2016.

LaBosse contacted me about a month ago from Bora Bora, Tahiti, saying that he was soon heading to France to visit family and friends, and to embrace once again the mystique of Marseilles with its stark reminder of the Count of Monte Cristo's just revenge, the Chateau d'if; and also the cosmopolitan boulevards of Paris. He was disappointed that he could only book passage on the TGV from Paris. In bygone days, the more calming, luxurious, and enjoyable mode of transportation was aboard Le Train Bleu - Wagon-lits, leaving Paris in the evening, and arriving to coffee and croissants served in your couchette compartment in the morning as the train glides along the Mediterranean shoreline heading east into the rays of the morning sun.

Raphael Hotel, Kansas City, Missouri
21 February 2019

LaBosse is here with me in Kansas City, Missouri, so that we can continue work on my story before he heads to France. He doesn't have a lot of time here, so we'll be continuing in other locations including Québec City.

LaBosse: Beau, I must say, I never thought we would be meeting in Kansas City. The is my first visit to this part of the United States. From what I can see, this city has some nice offerings. That was a nice Italian restaurant we ate at last night, and the breakfast here in the hotel was excellent. Of course, I know that sitting here in the Raphael is far removed from the hidden inner-city layers of poverty, inequality, and race issues that are a part of the cityscape of most, if not all American cities. What's up with Kansas City, why are you here?
Beau: Back in 2014, my son, Don Alonzo, was transferred here by his job. He was in airline management, and his position frequently required working long hours. At that time, he was a single dad with three children ages 5, 9, and 15, and he really needed help. And so, here I am. All that has changed now. The oldest is grown, and the younger ones, two girls, are living with their mom, and with him, separately, in Chicago. That all happened about a year ago. In the meantime, my wife has developed some commits here, and my will finish school in a few months. When all of this is done, I'll be saying goodbye to KCMO; that's how many refer to the city in Missouri. They call Kansas City, Kansas; KCK.

You've lived in many different cultures, and have acclimated without a problem, in fact, you thrive on people's differences and traditions. Without comparing, what say you about Kansas City? Lifestyle? Are you stimulated? Are you happy? Continue, sir!
I certainly don't want to offend Kansas Citians by saying this, but as I explain, I think most will agree, because my impressions have come directly from them in friendly conversations, and after thinking about it for a

moment, some will surely concur. Kansas City is the oddest place I've ever lived! And my opinion is based more on my lack of experience living in midwestern American culture, than anything else.

Please explain, odd.
I think in many ways Kansas City is a perfect example of the post-war *American Dream*. Like the 1950s TV shows: *Danny Thomas, Ozzie and Harriet;* and soap operas like *Search for Tomorrow, Guiding Light,* and others from that era that reflect the trials, tribulations, and complexities of life behind the white picket fence. For many here, life is between a job, the subdivision, and the mall. A life that eludes many aspects of peoples' own cultural heritage, and connectivity to that of others until it dissolves into near nothingness, passing through generations in suburbia. There's no connection, or very little, to the various ethnic groups in the area outside of eating at a Mexican restaurant, or having BBQ at one the Black owned restaurants, then maybe taking in some music in the *Jazz District,* which is a real adventure for some. All of this operating beneath a patina of fake fulfilment, and the comfort zone of the *American Dream.*

And as with anywhere, you have the wealthy elite who venture out all over the planet for business, pleasure, adventure, and so forth. For many of them, KC is a comfortable safe haven. The modus operandi for those who venture out seems to be to travel the world and enjoy the hospitality of other cultures. However, when they return, that international *joie de vivre* vanishes. They are not capable of the same hospitality that embraced them while travelling in Italy, France, Africa, or wherever. Here, they actually embrace what I call

Internal Xenophobia. Not only are they closed off to outsiders, the have concerns about interacting with people who live on which side of the Stateline, who are from a particular county, if someone is from north or south of the river, and so on. Some, not all, have an insular existence. And that's a word I've often heard to describe Kansas Citians by outsiders like me, and occasionally, by Kansas Citians themselves.

And the automobiles. This is almost totally an automobile culture. It's impossible to interact with people in your car. There's a great interstate highway system here, no doubt about it. And compared to most cities, the traffic is almost nothing, and what little there is doesn't last long. Only accidents prolong the commute, and many of those could be avoided if people would slow down, and not get high or drink and drive.

I think any highly social person would fine what you have described as odd, or very different from what they've come to enjoy over the years. But like you said, it would be unfair to compare. You're living in the American Midwest, the Bible belt.
Odd is not negative. It's odd to me because of the way the society is structured. I, and other outsiders that I've met find it very difficult to get to know people, even very casually; and I find it weird that many people seemed to live in a kind of mobile bubble that doesn't permit penetration to those outside of it. The numerous bubbles sometimes interact out of necessity, like at work or sporting events, but they rarely intertwine. There are defined boundaries here that are geographical, psychological, economic, and racial.

The KC metro and surrounding areas are segregated by design. At the root, as well as other racist tendencies endemic to Euro-American societies, is the thinking of developer, J. C. Nichols, who basically drew a road map, and with the help of other greedy, spineless, and racist motherfuckers, implemented a sinister plan of apartheid, red lining, and economic inequality. Quite literally, a highway, psychological walls, and street boundaries were built, and still exist for the purpose of keeping people of colour, and whites separated. The first time I drove through certain neighbourhoods, seriously, I thought I had mistakenly entered a movie set. I mean, I thought that maybe a film was being made about slave times, and the houses I saw were slave shacks. The more I drove, I began to see a variety of ramshackle houses; some of them sliding off the foundations, some with collapsing front porches and people sitting on them. This is indeed a dark and evil part of KC history. I could speak about this for a long time. It's an issue that is still going on that can't be treated lightly. I suggest are readers do a little online research into the life and practices of J. C. Nichols. It's quite a story of greed, and apartheid that was welcomed, and emulated by many real estate developers across America.

Knowing you, I'm sure you must have found a way to circumvent the insular KC status quo, right?
As I said, KC is about cars. Interestingly, there was a time when this was a model city for public transportation. There was an enviable light rail system that served the city and suburbs. Transportation experts from around the would come to study the KC transit system. As part of the *American Dream,* real estate developers, car manufacturers, oil companies, bankers and others eventually convinced people that they didn't have to rub

shoulders with people of colour and lesser means on trolleys, buses, and at terminals. They sought fulfilment and security in a suburban home in places like Prairie Village, Overland Park, Lee's Summit, and Brookside, or other areas without ever seeing a person of colour unless they were housekeepers, gardeners, or picking up the trash. And, in some dream homes, they could click open their garage door opener, enter, and never see or speak to their neighbours. Insulation. 1957, the last trolley ran in Kansas City. The inner-city communities were left without access to downtown and beyond. Downtown eventually became desolate as shops and department stores closed, and possibilities for employment ceased to exist. The post-war *White America Dream* had taken hold in Kansas City.

Let's fall back, then forward. I arrived here in October of 2014. *The Kansas City Royals* baseball team were in the World Series but lost. In 2015 they won the World Series. It was truly amazing what happened to the spirit of the city. Strangers were hugging, dancing together, sharing drinks in the streets, jubilation everywhere. It had been years since the Royals had won the championship.

I decided to experiment. I had a pretty nice car, a Honda Crosstour that was roomy and well appointed. I signed to drive with a rideshare company.

You're kidding. Man, you didn't tell me. You been tight lipped on that one. We met in Québec and Iceland, and you never hinted at your experiment. We've spoken by phone countless times! You're good!
Ah yes. In fact, right now is the very first time I've men-

tioned it to anyone. I mean for the experiment to work I had to operate in complete secrecy. Honestly, that's one of the great lessons I learned from you, LaBosse, secrecy.

And so, I begin learning about my surroundings, and the people who live here. After about a month I realized that it wouldn't take long for me to learn a great deal more about the area than some natives. Driving took me absolutely everywhere without reservation. I had no paranoid myths going on in my head about state lines, and county lines, and so on. I met really fine Kansas City residents from all walks of life including writers, lawyers, medical professionals, and shameless hussies. I met women in their early thirties coming from a wedding reception who were in tears because they were not yet married. More than once, I was a comforter and counsellor in very volatile and emotional situations with riders. I never knew about the pressure in some families for women to marry and have children. That's a big deal in some elements of Bible Belt culture. And the hypocrisy. A few Bloody Mary's on a plane can really loosen lips. From time-to-time I'd ferry home a cheating spouse who was returning from a business trip. My, my, such stories of lust and deceit! It was always amusing, and sometimes sad to see the eager children rushing out of the house to greet their mom or dad. I've even been given guilty-hush money. Tips that were so large it had to be that. And sometimes there was a large gratuity just for keeping silent and listening. And this is when rideshare companies had no tipping on the app, so I got cash and sometimes checks.

Being in service is unique in many ways. There are some that you serve who rarely see you as an equal. If you meet some people, let's say, at a vernissage, and you were close friends with the artist or gallery director, and you shared some of your life stories over drinks they'd be kissing your ass and eager to get to know you. Now drive the same people, share the same stories, and they think that in some way, you're inferior to them. I was amused by the arrogance that goes along with the perceived opportunity to be in charge of another person. There were some laughable white privilege encounters. Here's an example: I went to pick up some folks on wealthy Ward Parkway. There were five passengers who wanted to get in, but my car only seats five in total. I politely explained that I'm not insured if I have more people in the car than there are seat belts, and I tell them to call another car. Man, you should have heard the threats and proclamations. 'We're white, just drive and don't worry about it!' Then they got in anyway. Four white frat-type boys all over each other in the back seat, and the drunk-ass fool who ordered the ride in the front. I told them I wasn't going a damn inch. Now, I wasn't so polite. I wasn't going to let them commandeer my car.

That situation could have turned very bad quickly. Part of our ongoing survival training is to diffuse this type of bullshit before things get out of hand, or the bad behaviour guys, because they're white, will make it look like you're doing something to them. We have been there! What did you do?
I asked the guy in seat next to me if that was his house where they got in. It was a huge mansion, and he said it was his home. I told him that in a few minutes the police were going to show up because I had pushed the driver assistance button on my phone when they started arguing. I said that this situation is about to be-

come embarrassing in a few minutes, but not for me because I don't give a fuck, I'm following the rules. Then he and his boys cursed a little and got out. I drove off. Police didn't come because at that time there was no emergency feature on the driver app. Now, these situations were extremely rare, but you know, sometimes things happen.

That's pretty good. I'd imagine this kind of behaviour is more likely at night or on weekends.
Definitely. Night driving on a regular basis wasn't my thing anyway. Passengers were generally pretty cool, just out for a good time. If there's a concern about night driving, it's really the drunk drivers out on the roads. They are the problem. From time-to time, if there was a convention or some other event that brought in out-of-towners, I'd do some night driving.

What else stands out in your driving experiment?
Well, from riders, I learned about some interesting Kansas City folklore. There's an area called the *West Bottoms,* where there are old warehouses, some of which have been converted to residential and office spaces. Legend has it that during prohibition, there were a number of murders between rival gangs who were battling each other for control of the illegal liquor business, and shipments of all sorts of contraband on the Missouri river. Murder in and around these warehouses was quite common. I met a few people who claimed the *West Bottoms* are haunted, and some claim they have seen ghost on certain streets and rising up out of the river. There's a ghost museum, there's a haunted building called *The Beast,* that really packs them in especially during Halloween; and there's *The Edge of Hell* haunted building. Some people come out

from these places trembling and visibly shaken. There are many event spaces down there for damn near everything from weddings to wild-ass parties. Seems people like the idea of being in a ghost inhabited area. There's live music, good restaurants, art galleries, wine bars, espresso bars, summer festivals, and whatever else they can think of to really keep the area thriving.

You really needed to know what's happening for your experiment to work. I mean if you set out to something that really isn't your thing, you still have to be the best that you can be.
Exactly! And I became the best of the best. That ain't me just saying that about me, it's what others have said in in the app's passenger comment section.

Do you have any closing thoughts on Kansas City before we move on?
Kansas City is a city that's reinventing itself. It takes time, and inspiring leaders to realize the dream for KC that a lot of planners have. Younger, energetic, and creative entrepreneurs and others envision an International City at the crossroads of the USA. I think Kansas City is the best convention city I've ever seen in the Midwest. Visitors who come here are treated well and are offered many options for enjoying the city. There's the *Negro Leagues Baseball Museum,* that has a fantastic presentation, *The Jazz Museum*, that honours Kansas City's vibrant Jazz past, the past that I was somewhat disappointed not to find when I moved here. No more *Charlie Parker* and *Ben Webster* types, like those cats and other greats, they've died or moved away. And there are great restaurants that specialize in Barbecue, one of the city's oldest dining traditions. I think once the new international airport is completed, Kansas City will

become the international capital of the Midwest, as well as the USA's major crossroads. And I must add, In my opinion Kansas City is the weddings capital of the U.S., I've never seen anything like it. Not shotgun weddings, but full-blown ceremonies with receptions, pre-parties, the works. From March to November, wedding madness. I was thinking of setting up a drive-thru wedding and divorce business, offering simple weddings and no-fault divorces.

There will always be suburbia, but that's not vitality. That's not hearing other languages being spoken on the streets by visitors, and some residents. That's not raising children outside of a bubble. That's not a light rail that will eventually connect neighbourhoods, and with any luck, the sports venues. And that would really be good because now people go to sports events, drink, then drive home. If the driving intoxicated laws were enforced, there wouldn't be enough people able to drive to and from Chiefs and Royals games; they would all be in the drunk tank. Trains to the sports venues would be a big plus, and unlike being in a car, total strangers could interact. I think that would be a big step toward dissolving the geographical and psychological boundaries that exist here.

This certainly has been a different experience for you. I think you've done very well to be in a holding pattern.
Holding pattern indeed. Here, when I mention that I've traveled any place outside of the U.S., 90 percent of people ask if I traveled because I was in the military. I mean a lot of these people can't imagine going someplace because that's what you want to do, not because you were ordered to do so. This is not Rome, Barce-

lona, Dakar, or any cosmopolitan hub, where the first day in town I was having coffee with total strangers or travellers like myself. This place is about familiarity. If you're an outsider, that's your place here unless you put in a lot of time. I rather like 'outsider' status.

I think Kansas City has a great future. Kansas City has a Black mayor, *Sly James,* who has really given a lot of focus to progressive ideas. He seems to be frequently in conflict with the old guard, but has enough support to get things done, like the new trolley system, and the building of a new, truly international airport. Because of term limits, Sly will be unable to run for mayor again. There's buzz about who will replace Sly. To me though, one candidate stands out because of his community involvement, broad vision, and experiences outside of Kansas City including extensive travel. That person is also Black, *Quintin Lucas.* I think he may be good for Kansas City.

That's uncharacteristically supportive coming from you. I know you have real disdain for politicians. I remember your advice, 'If you don't like pee-pee, and you wanna keep your money, stay away from politicians and preachers.'
Ha-ha! Right, that's true. But I shouldn't be blinded by my own distaste for the manipulative cultures of politicians and preachers. There are exceptions, or maybe I should say, exceptions are possible even though I've never met any. I think Lucas is cool. He is from Kansas City and has the kind of broad background that I generally admire in people. He has lived in Cape Town, South Africa, and has travelled extensively. He is seriously committed to community, and lives in the historical Jazz District. I ain't tooting his horn, he is young, in

his thirties, progressive, well-educated, and not one of the old guard. We'll see, or should I say, Kansas Citians will see. I hear my name being called by the South Pacific.

I know that's right! I know you are missing the bord de mer, and some other delights. Have you any additional closing comments?
I want to mention a happenstance that has added pleasure to my sojourn. I was driving around one day and heard some Blues on the radio. And that was unusual because I rarely listen to radio. On this day I was trying to find some news when I heard Chicago Blues artist, Otis Rush, being played on a local station. I contacted the show host, a gentleman by the name of *Jason Vivone,* who turned out be a fine guitarist, bandleader, and someone with a real passion and knowledge of the Blues. Sometimes I sit-in with him and his partner, *Paula Crawford,* who plays rhythm guitar. Always lots of fun to be on stage with them. Also, I do manage to escape from time-to-time to see family in Toronto and do some playing with my old friend from Paris, *Jean-François Fabiano,* in Montréal, where I also have many friends, some who I've known for over fifty years. Also, my daughter and I have had some travel breaks to Vancouver, Seattle, San Francisco, Reykjavik, Québec City, and London. And lastly, I keep some aspects of my brain in order by teaching writing classes at *Harper College* in Palatine, Illinois.

Moving on. Five years ago back in Reykjavik you said you wanted to speak about time you spent in Switzerland, and a few other places. Then we fast forwarded to Chicago a few years onward so you could share some aspects of the Chicago Blues scene that you became a part of as a performer, producer, and magazine publisher. How should we proceed today? Where is your head at?
I've been thinking a lot about Geneva, Switzerland. For the most part, my life there was not enjoyable. In summer 1972, I went to Geneva to study music at the *Conservatoire de Genève,* and checkout a new scene.

I arrived from Paris by train. Almost immediately things started happening. I decided to stroll up the street to the right of, and across the street from the train station. I came across a small record store, *Disco-Club,* that was within five minutes of the station. I entered the store and greeted the shopkeeper who was the only person in the store. I began perusing the Jazz and Blues section and found a couple of records I had made with Archie Shepp. The shopkeeper was looking at me, but not as though he was worried about me stealing, or threatening him in some way, as I had become used to growing up in the United States. No, his look was more a look of curiosity, as though he was trying to place my face with one of those hundreds of Black music albums. I sensed his curiosity, and spoke: 'Man, you really have an amazing collection here!' I said, hoping he understood my English. And he did. 'Merci!' he said. The Swiss often say merci, when responding to English, Swiss German, and Romansh. And then he introduced himself as Paul Meyer, the owner of the shop, and I introduced myself. Paul was quite pleased that I came to his shop. Well, we spoke at great length about music, life in Geneva, and my intentions. I knew right away, without a doubt, Paul was a good man. I asked for recommendations about finding a hotel, and eventually the best way to go about finding an apartment. Paul asked me if I'd like to stay at his place until I found an apartment. He also said he could introduce me to people who could be of help. Now Paul wasn't a young cat. I'm guessing he was around fifty, and me, I was twenty-three. I accepted Paul's offer and spent the next several nights at his house. Paul was a gracious host. He had visitors almost nightly, so I met all kinds of people. And when he wasn't entertaining, he was visiting friends, and invited me along. In less than a week I met people in the music business, finance people, lovely ladies. During the day I would explore the city, the café scene, and eventually I also get myself enrolled in the conservatory.

After about a week, Paul introduced me to a wonderful lady from New York, Betsy Cathro. Betsy had a spacious apartment with a room to rent in the same building as Migros food store near Place de Neuve, which is where the Conservatory was located. Betsy and I hit it off instantly. Betsy over the next weeks introduced me into her various circles that included people from across the planet. That's one of the characteristics of Switzerland, a lot of different people, and many with lots of money.

Geneva has always been a highly social town with lots of financial people, celebrities, diplomats, and others.
The city serves as part-time home to many. A place to do business, a place to romp, a place where indiscretions not allowed in some people's native cultures, like

the US bible belt, or perhaps some parts of the middle east, flourish and go unnoticed. I recall fun evenings at the *Griffins Club* partying with people from across the globe and the Swiss jet set.

I remember one night there with you. At the next table were *Victor Herbert,* a very close associate of *Bernie Cornfeld,* and several other people, mostly beautiful ladies, who had been associated with *IOS, Investors Overseas Services,* at some point. Joe, the manager, and good friend intentionally seated us next to the IOS table and made introductions. Joe made a point of highlighting my music during his introduction. Lively conversation ensued.

Oh yes! That was a fun evening that included dancing, champagne toasts to everything including the good old days of IOS, Bernie Cornfeld and his bevy of babes, the beautiful legs of the women present, the insane amounts of money that had all made and spent, and to you, Beau, they saluted your artistry.
I was touched by their acknowledgement of my music, and further touched by Simone, a vivacious musical genius who was seated with the IOS party, and very near to us.

I recall Simone, an opera singer who asked you to help her learn to sing Jazz. She was fascinated with Lambert, Hendricks, and Ross.
Right. I encouraged her to keep listening, and to think about translating songs from English into French, as a means of putting her own soul into her renditions, and also to introduce the music to her fan base. She was really a special lady. Not only beautiful, but she had an incredible knowledge of music and theatre. Her per-

formance repertoire included amazing contrast from *Carmina Burana* to *Edith Piaf.* Unfortunately, she was affianced to a wealthy gentleman from Lugano who was away on business in Singapore. I did not pursue her, and that was the right decision because my life would probably have become far too complicated.

From what you've mentioned in the past, you're probably right; but then again, who knows what course your life would have taken had you pursued her. One can only guess.
That's right. I met Victor Herbert and those IOS hangers-on in 1972. And you know that IOS crowd was pretty fast moving, a lot of dealings in a lot of directions. In 1973, Bernie Cornfeld spent nearly a year in a Swiss prison after his IOS mutual fund company collapsed. He was accused of swindling and fraud. He was later acquitted. Bernie's problems continued, as well as his lavish lifestyle. In retrospect, even though I was certainly attracted to some aspects of IOS culture, I'm glad I didn't get personally, or to deeply involved with any of the people.

Bernie Cornfeld's story is incredibly interesting, and exciting to read about. I think our readers should checkout a book called: 'do you sincerely want to be rich?' *The Full Story of Bernard Cornfeld and IOS,* by Charles Raw, Bruce Page & Godfrey Hodgson; Library of Larceny, Broadway Books, New York, 1971.

Also, there is an absolutely intriguing, continuing Blog-Memoir titled: T*he Amazing Life and Times of Edward Carter – Unique Entrepreneur.* Chapter four details Carter's extensive work with IOS; and his own dalliances and adventures around the world

Intriguing, the world of get rich quick schemes, Ponzi schemes, etc., and there are a lot of legit operations, but the more you make, the more scrutiny. Moving on, how were things rolling for you after you got more settled?

I was living with Betsy and studying piano and solfège at the Conservatoire. Things were going well, smooth, and easy with time on my hands. Paul Meyer continued introducing me into various circles including people outside of Geneva in Lausanne, Lugano, Zurich, and Zermatt. I spent time in *Zino Davidoff's* cigar store on Rue du Marché, without a doubt, the finest shop in the world for cigars, and exquisite smokers' requisites.

The days drifted by, and I indulged in activities befitting my gift of magnetically attracting ladies. In those days I played a bit of Chess, but not well. From time-to-time I would go to the *Cafe du Bourg-de-Four* in *Vieux Genève.* Though not a Chess establishment per se, occasionally patrons would play. Early one evening I was seated at a table on the rather small terrace. Next to me sat a young man setting up Chess pieces. In his distinctly, non-distinct American accent, he invited me to play. I say non-distinct because people from say, Boston, the Bronx, Louisiana, and some other places have distinct accents, whereas folks from the San Fernando Valley or Hollywood do not, not unless they brought it with them from somewhere else. My guess was that this gentleman was probably from California.

I told him that I enjoyed the game, but that I was by no means accomplished. In fact, I was far from competitive even at the most rudimentary of levels. But I agreed to play on the condition that my back wasn't facing the street, *Place du Bourg-du-Four.* You know, some old habits don't fade away, I'm from Chicago and I ain't turning my back to no street!

I know that's right. Same rules apply, could be Compton, Harlem, Ibiza, or Genève. One should face the scene. How did you get on with your opponent?
He laughed at my request but agreed. His back was facing the Place. I told him not to worry if some shit went down, I had his back, from the front. We laughed. More than anything though, this young white man in his mid-twenties was curious as to what I, a young Black man with an obvious Black inner city, post reconstruction accent, I doubt if he thought that through, was doing in Geneva, Switzerland. And so, he asked, and I told him that I was there for studies and other matters.

Certainly, he wanted to know about the other matters, right?
Well, I just reversed that shit. Even though I knew Switzerland was crawling with foreigners, I pretended that I found it strange that he was there. I said I had met only a few Americans, which was not true, and that I was delighted to make his acquaintance, which was true. And I asked him to tell me about his presence. And at that point we introduced ourselves to one another.

He said is name is *Wes Holden,* and I introduced myself as Lincoln, pointing out that friends call me Beau, and as a musician, I'm called Chicago Beau. We shook hands, and we started our game. This was a long dragged-out game. Many of his friends dropped by. He ordered drinks and socialized. He bought me drinks, I bought him drinks. He introduced me to people. Then his brother, Scott, popped by. After a couple of hours, the game was coming to a close. Checkmate, he won. Finally, I thought, my concentration had totally dissipated due to all of the activity and socializing.

The drinks flowed, and the simultaneous conversations became livelier and more animated. Everyone wanted to know who Wes' new friend was, and he told them, and we all had fun. After a while, another gentleman arrived, and someone got up and gave him their seat immediately. It was quite a respectful gesture, I thought. The man looked familiar. I was thinking, I know this face, I recognize the walk and voice, I just could not recall who he might be. Then West introduced me. He said, 'Mr. Beau, this is my dad, the legendary Hollywood leading man, and tough guy, William Holden.' There was praise and contempt in his voice. We shook hands. I recalled him from a film I had seen recently, Sam Peckinpah's, *The Wild Bunch,* where he led a gang of aging bandits on train and bank robberies in the early 1900s, and a final bloody shootout with the Mexican army that damn near everybody got killed including Holden's gang.

By now the small café terrace is packed, and the night crowd ebbs and flows in and out. Dinner is being served and multiple languages and laughter can be heard. Right?
Yes, my kind of groove! Well, William Holden didn't stay long, maybe thirty minutes. He got picked up by a lady and they drove off. Wes and I continued talking with each other and other people. Geneva is not a huge city, and a lot of circles overlap. I soon discovered that several people I had previously met, knew people that I was meeting.

That's a characteristic of an open city. One just has to learn how to navigate the different circles and learn which ones to avoid for whatever reasons. Now that you're making acquaintances, did any stronger or more defining relationships form?

At the time I met Wes, I'd been in Geneva just over a month, and already had met several nice ladies. Paul Meyer introduced me to Eva, a student from Sierra Leone, we hung out for a bit. Then suddenly, out of nowhere it seemed, her designated fiancé showed up from Freetown. Apparently, Eva's father and the fiancé's father had made this arrangement, and they both were concerned about Eva being alone in Geneva. And so, that was that.

Shortly thereafter, Betsy introduced me to Adriana Le Comte, a painter and dancer. We hit it off immediately. At the time Adriana was kind of a part-time love of an attorney named Igor. Igor was older than Adriana, maybe he was around fifty, Adriana and I were the same age. Igor was quite successful, and from what I could tell, indulged himself in numerous part-time liaisons. Probably, Adriana was doing the same, so my presence was not interference, it was just part of the status quo.

Adriana lived in a huge apartment located on Rue de Lancy in Carouge, and independent Municipality bordering Geneva. Igor owned the building, but he didn't live there. He had an exquisite house elsewhere. After part-timing myself with Adriana for about a month, we decided to try and live together. At some point Adriana introduced me to Igor, and he suggested that if I wanted to find a more permanent space than Betsy's, he had several properties that I might find suitable. At that time, he didn't know that Adriana and I were getting casual. I told Adriana that if we were going to try a do a thing together, she should let Igor know. I didn't think she should break off her friendship, I wanted them to end the physical part. So, Adriana went to Igor's one evening to give him the news. The following morning, Adriana rang and said that Igor wasn't terribly upset, just more surprised than anything; and that he wished us well. I thought Adriana's actions may have brought Igor some relief, as I'm sure he was part-timing with ladies pretty much to full capacity. I mean one person can only handle so much. I moved from Betsy's to Adriana's in Carouge within a few days. The timing was right for my transition, as I didn't want to wear out my welcome with Betsy. Also, Betsy had a very jealous, nervous, and insecure boyfriend, Jean M, who, on several occasions nearly provoked me enough to kick his fool ass; however, I didn't want to spend any time in a Swiss jail.

Okay. Now you and Adriana are an item. No part-timing by either one of you. Y'all are going on into the sunset?
That was the plan. But LaBosse, let me tell you, I no idea what I was in for. No Idea!

Je sais c'est dificile, mais, commence. Let it roll!
Adriana and I, we are inseparable for weeks at a time. We are never bored with each other's company. We were out and about, we had dinner parties, and we were invited to parties. One Sunday afternoon I was invited to her family home, which was in a high-rise apartment building in a posh Geneva neighbourhood. Adriana's family was coldly welcoming. You know, forced politeness as to not hurt Adriana's feelings. Adriana had an older brother, Carlo, who by far was the

most conversant, and one could see that he and Adriana got on well. The fiftyish parents on the other hand were robotic towards each other. The mom, Gertrude was Swiss German with a harsh pale face; and the Swiss Italian dad, Pietro, was equally as bland even when he forced a smile. I doubt if either one of them had encountered a Black person before. I decided to break the ice by talking about how much I loved Geneva, and how fortunate I was to be going to the Conservatoire. I added that I had met Adriana through mutual friends. Then Adriana picked up the conversation that was now going on in French, German, Italian, and English. As all this conversation was going on, I studied the family's interactions and vibes with each other. You didn't have to be a psychologist to see the strain and pain between the mother and father, and the same between mother and daughter.

Carlo told me that their parents were not on the best of terms. At this point their marriage and family life were solely for the sake of their children, and for appearances in the community. Pietro was a successful builder of commercial and residential properties, from shopping complexes to apartments like the one his family lived in. Anyway, Adriana and I announced our wedding plans. The parents seemed a bit taken aback, while the brother was congratulatory. And then came the expected questions. Are you sure? Have you thought about the seriousness? Where are you going to live?

As the evening progressed with coffee and sweets, the family, Le Comte, loosened up a bit. I told them about my family. About my dad being an attorney, and they seemed quite impressed with that. Of course, I discussed my goals as a professional musician, and to eventually become a music producer. But I stressed that nothing was etched in stone. I mean I was twenty-three years old, and inwardly, I didn't have a clue. The main thing in my mind was just to keep growing and develop some possibilities that Adriana and I could do together. You know, our situation was like the song, *Young and In Love*. Nothing else mattered.

Sounds like a really strained evening all around.
It was. And Adriana told me that her mother had a few not so nice comments to say to her, including the embarrassment the family would suffer because of marriage to a Black man. She went as far as to say that the marriage could have a negative impact on her dad's business. Adriana's normally cheerful demeanour waned over the next couple of weeks. We spoke about it, and she said she was disappointed by her parents, but not totally surprised by their concern or possible rejection of her choices.

In Switzerland before marriage, the couple must post Banns, a notification of intent to marry, at the civil registrar's office. The waiting time can be lengthy as time is needed for anyone with a valid objection to come forward. Usually, the only objection is that one or both of the engaged may already be married. We were both in the clear on that one.

As our wedding day drew nearer, Adriana became more disturbed. She became distant, almost never speaking. I sensed that there was something going on inside her that was deeply troubling. When she did speak what she said sometimes made no sense. At times she slurred as though she had been drugged. Then she would snap out of it, and maybe say she was just thinking about her family, or more specifically, her father. One day I came home to home to find her seated at her drawing table covered in India ink.

Covered! As in her full body?
Ink was running down the front of her white linen Greek style dress. Ink covered her face and ran from her mouth. She appeared to have drunk some ink. I asked her what was happening, and she was completely incoherent, making no sense. And she was in and out tears and moaning I got her cleaned up and got her to lay down. She was like a limp zombie. Eyes just staring blankly into nowhere.

I called her uncle, Marco, Pietro's brother and explained what was happening. He told me to hold on, keep an eye on her, and that he would come soon. In less than an hour he showed up. 'Adriana! Adriana!' he called to her. She just looked at him, and kind of beyond him, into the distance, with eyes red from crying.

Marco said we were going to take Adriana for treatment at a psychiatric hospital call the *La Metairie* in Nyon. La-Bosse, up until that point in my life I had never experienced such sadness. I mean the woman that I loved had apparently suffered some type of devastating mental breakdown, and it was in some way tied to her family, and seemingly at this point, something to do with her father. I was thinking that perhaps her family had taken a firm position against the marriage, and that maybe the father had threatened her in some way. I didn't know anything for sure at this point except that she was suffering, I was concerned and suffering, and somewhat oddly, her uncle seemed prepared for such an event, to the point of very quickly making arrangements at the *La Metairie.* I assumed that this was not her first visit, and that he knew, but wasn't saying what Adriana may have been suffering from, or the causes

The drive to Nyon took about an hour. During the trip Marco asked me questions that I sure he already knew the answers. Bullshit like, what did I think happened, and had she been taking drugs or drinking or drinking a lot? I told him to stop with the questions. The woman I love is a zombie next to me in the back seat. I'm holding tightly on to a person who is starring into space because he told me to do so because she may try and jump out if the car. I told Marco that he had to know what was up with Adriana. I told me she had been quite concerned about her father's thoughts on the marriage, to the points of bursting into tears more than once. The only thing this motherfucker had to say was that we'll have to wait and see what the doctors have to say.

When we arrived at the reception desk, Adriana was immediately taken away in a wheelchair. There was no check in, or questions asked to me by doctors or anyone. I was given the name of a person to call after 10 days, and they took my number. The Metairie people already had the Le Comte family's details.

LaBosse, this was painful. If you take a loved on to the cemetery, you know it's permanent. One may never recover from the pain. In the case if taking Adriana to a mental hospital, I felt even though she was alive, I may never know this person again. And that's what happened. Gradually and permanently.

For certain this was not Adriana's first visit. You surely had questions for Marco on the way back to Geneva.
Marco was tight lipped. He said that Adriana had psychological issues in the past, but he was not specific. I asked why he had come for Adriana rather than her dad or mother. His response was strange but revealing. He said that they were occupied with some family business. I knew this was BS. I suggested that Adriana didn't really want to see her parents. He nodded in agreement. I got the picture, there was definitely some family shit going on, probably some family taboo shit that had really damaged Adriana. I didn't press him anymore. He dropped me at home in Carouge, and I begin the process of sorting out my love for Adriana and the complications with her family; as well thinking hard about getting my life back on track.

How long before you saw Adriana again?
It was around five or six weeks. And during that time all kinds of things happened ranging from peace and calm to anger and madness. A lot of people, friends of Adriana and myself were deeply concerned. Especially the women. One of Adriana's friends, whose nickname was Mousie because she was so tiny in stature with a tiny voice. She was a good friend of Adriana and knew some of her deepest secrets. One day she asked me if Adriana had mentioned anything about her dad. I said she hadn't but to me it seemed strange that the closer are marriage date came, the more she was concerned about his thoughts. That seemed normal enough, but her concerns brought on tears, arguments over the phone with her mother in German which I didn't understand, and finally, descent into the state that she was in when we took her to the hospital. Mousie said that

she believed that Adriana felt that she was betraying her father by getting married, and furthermore, he was not too accepting of her marriage to a Black man. I pressed Mousie for more specific details, but she wouldn't divulge anything else. Could be that she didn't know any more, or she just couldn't bring herself to say more. I suspected that at some point Adriana's dad had done something to her sexually.

Given that neither the mother or father went with their child to *La Metairie*, I would say that they were definitely trying to avoid any kind of confrontation with Adriana, or people at the hospital.
Exactly. I had more than a hunch about what might have been, but at this point I had no proof. Like I said, her female friends expressed concern about her condition, but the males responses ranged from indifference, to accusing me of having given her drugs. You know, the old stereotype of Black musicians being on drugs. Some said shit like, 'She was fine until she met you, what did you do to her?' Yea, before she met me, she partied a lot, and whatever that entailed, is how many knew her. But when she got serious, they thought something was wrong, and of course the only thing that could be wrong was something that was the result of her being with a Black man.

I know what you mean. Essentially, people like for things to stay the same. You're cool until you upset their norm. And with Adriana being in the hospital, there's no telling what might be revealed, including who may be implicated in whatever!
About a week after Adriana was in the hospital, out of the blue, her father got in touch and asked me if I would like to have a lunch. I suspected that he was curious

about her friends' concerns, you know, the buzz about her health.

I agreed to meet. He was extremely calm. Too calm, like he had taken something to assure his calmness. He asked if I had heard anything from the hospital. I had. They said they would let me know when they thought it would be okay to visit. I asked him the same thing. He had the same answer, however, I pressed him on why neither he or his wife went with her, or Marco and me to the hospital. He said that Adriana sometimes had serious anger issues, especially towards her parents and that he didn't want to exacerbate whatever issues that had necessitated her being taken to the hospital. I thought, well explained, put probably a bold-face lie.

Pietro asked me if I had needs like money or a new apartment. He asked me about my residency status in Switzerland. I told him that Adriana and I had not decided where we wanted to live, and for the moment I had no intention of leaving Geneva. I was thinking of applying for permanent residency. At that time, the first step was applying for, and getting approved for a Permis B, which required a sponsor and money. I forget how much money, but It was more than what I had. Pietro told me not to worry because he would take care of everything. The next time we met a few days later he gave me an envelope with lots of cash, I don't remember how much, and he told me to put him as a sponsor when I made my application. I banked the Swiss Francs, made my application, and after a short period of time I was issued a *Permis B* that allowed me to stay in Switzerland, and that was a step towards citizenship if I so desired.
And seeing Adriana?

Around a month into her hospitalization Adriana agreed to see me. I took a train to Nyon and a taxi to *La Metairie.* I had to walk down a long corridor and pass through several locked doors before I arrived in the area where Adriana was. She was heavily medicated but seemed happy to see me. The way she spoke was kind of in and out of reality. She told me things about certain patients that were clearly fantasy. For example, she said one fellow was the King of Corsica, and was there vacationing, and another lady was able to levitate. Then she would address something relevant like her dislike for her mother or speak kindly about her brother. When I asked about her father, she didn't want to speak about him.

There was surely something with her father, right?
Yes. I suspected something but didn't want to jump to conclusions. On my next visit, Adriana seemed more stable, and she agreed to see her father. Her doctors determined that she had been sufficiently medicated and in therapy enough to be able to manage a visit with him, but not her mother. As far as I know her mother never visited. And that's some strange shit!

Pietro and I went to Nyon together. After passing through the corridor, we arrived at Adriana's ward. She ran to greet her father, and when they embraced, he rubbed and fondled her left breast in a manner that revealed that what was happening was a matter of habit between them. The touching of his daughter in that manner confirmed my suspicions: that Pietro had been having sexual encounters with Adriana and given the ease of his behaviour, I figured it had been going on for a long time.

Good Lord, man! Did you maintain your cool? If you

did, it must have been difficult.
Well, I was cool, but also angry. I didn't respond mainly because I knew Adriana was in a fragile condition. I basically let them visit, I didn't have much to say of any importance. Pietro thought that I was responsible for Adriana agreeing to see him. He was somewhat correct; I had asked about seeing him when we had phone conversations. But also, weeks of taking medications and therapy was working.

After about eight weeks Adriana was released from La Metairie. Adriana was released to her uncle. He and I picked her up and brought her to the apartment in Carouge. I knew that things would never be the same. I knew that what we had was over, and that she probably would never completely recover from the trauma being truly in love had caused. The first night she Adriana was back we went out to dinner, and it was at this dinner that she revealed that her father had sexually abused her since she was nine years old. She had become used to it. She said she really didn't understand how she could make love to any man other than her father. She had many lovers in the past, was never in love with any of them. But with me, she was in love, and getting married was definitely a betrayal of her father. And her mother, of course she knew, but never said anything.

And not to digress, but since then I've seen similar scenarios repeated several times. The mother wants her security. She knows her husband or boyfriend is abusing her child or children but lives in total denial. And some of them to the point of accusing their molested children of lying or being jealous. But back to Adriana, I couldn't see where her therapy did anything more than enable her to cope and live in some kind of state of acceptance.

If I'm reading you correctly, you're saying she was not well. They just put a band-aid on her wounds. The real issue had not been dealt with, right?
That's right. The motherfucking issue with her that's endemic in that society, and many others, Is that they treat the symptoms, but not that cause, which may be impossible to treat in certain circumstances. Motherfucking molesters should be locked away, and not have their sicknesses managed in group therapy, or family therapy. Give the abusers therapy, but in jail. I'm sure in some cases that may happen. But there's lots of money around, and the people who have it, along with their sick and sinister ways, can keep themselves out of jail for years, you know, a lifetime.

How did you manage the changes that were occurring?
While Adriana was in Nyon I occupied myself by writing, hanging out at the *Griffins Club*, and going to dinner parties. It was at one of those dinner parties that I met Sigrid, a very clear-headed and attractive Black woman. During our initial conversation I learned that her mother was a well-known clinical psychologist with a practice in Geneva. Her mother, Constance Rose, was from Chicago, and her life's adventures had taken her to numerous destinations. Sigrid was maybe twenty years old at the time, and very happy to meet a Black person from Chicago, as she had been mostly raised in Europe and had known only a few Black people from the United States outside of her mother's family who visited from time to time.

It seems the Cosmics were looking out for you, and

Sigrid and Constance came into your life at the right time.
For sure. And this was certainly a time when I needed some relief from the stress of dealing with Adriana and her family. To be in the presence of this energetic, and beautiful sister was healing, and her mother being a psychologist with a practice in Geneva would prove to be of great benefit. I told Sigrid an abbreviated version about my relationship with Adriana, her family, and what had occurred. The next day I met Constance and we had a lengthy conversation about everything over a bottle of wine. What great good fortune to have met her! Constance's practice primarily dealt with the problems, and neuroses that seemed to plague the Swiss social orders, from the wealthy to the working class, from children to parents, from broken homes to the semblance of family values rooted in Christian values. And she was perceived as an outsider; and that is what she was. She was humble and nonthreatening to her clients. She said her clients found it much easier to confide in her than her Swiss counterparts. That's quite understandable, they didn't have to worry about familiarity and leaks in a relatively small community.

After a few visits with Adriana at *La Metairie,* I convinced her and her doctors to let Constance come and visit. Constance became Adriana's regular counsellor after her release from the hospital. In fact, they developed a lengthy relationship that greatly helped Adriana's situation. I say situation because unlike a physical illness that may have a permanent cure, Adriana had to learn how to manage pain, suffering, and the realities of her family and heritage that would never go away.

When Adriana was released to you and Marco, was

everything arranged for continuing therapy?
Exactly. The next day after she was back in the apartment in Carouge, Constance made a home visit to see Adriana. Like I said, I knew things would never be the same, and I didn't pretend like they could be. My concern now was that Adriana continued stabilizing and that she was in good hands insofar her treatment and therapy was concerned. I felt like that was the case.

Within days Adriana moved out of our apartment and into an apartment owned by her brother in old Geneva. I have to admit the truth, I was relieved. The insanity, and pain was becoming too much to bear. I was worried about Adriana being alone, thankfully, she was all right and often in the company of her long-time friends, and she had frequent interactions with Constance.

How often did you see Adriana?
After Adriana was released from *La Metairie*, just a few times. Along with some of her friends and her brother, I helped her move into her new apartment. I saw her a couple of times with Constance. We had dinner together as I mentioned earlier, when she said she her father had been sexual with her since the age of nine. And I visited her once in her new apartment. After that, twenty years would pass before I would see her again. That was when I was on tour with The Art Ensemble of Chicago as part of their Tradition of Chicago Blues Tour on July 7, 1993, in Geneva. That was exactly twenty years ago to the month since I had seen Adriana.

How was your meeting after twenty years?
It was really a pleasure being with her. Adriana had read about the upcoming concert in Geneva and had contacted the concert organizers. They told me about the

contact and had arranged for her to come by the sound-check. Our visit went well. A lot had happened in both of our lives. Adriana had a teenage daughter and had been married and divorced. Her father had passed away. She said parapsychology was her profession. I did not ask about the depth or scope of her practice. She also said, "You did this to me." I interpreted that to mean that it was our relationship twenty years before that had triggered her confrontation with the truth, and further drama and misery with her family. Neither one of us really wanted to speak too much about the past. We spoke about our children, music, and life at the moment.

Was the meeting healing in some way?
I don't think healing happened. More than anything we reaffirmed the difficulty of trying to understand the workings of our minds, and emotions. I looked at her, listened to her, and asked myself, what is sanity? Something that is fixed or fixable. Yes and no. There are no parameters or boundaries. Solutions, if any, are often temporary. We agreed that this was a bright, and needed moment, and that we very well may not see each other for another twenty years, or not at all. That's what happened, we never, saw each other, or spoke again after the concert. Adriana passed in 2010. Into the mystic. Sail on!

Was this your first trip back to Geneva since you left back in '73?
Yes, it was. I also had a visit with Constance, and we reminisced a bit, but mostly caught up about current stuff. Constance's practice was thriving, and Sigrid, her daughter had moved to the U.S., and started a family. That was also a good and final visit.

A bit of sad news was that my old friend Paul Meyer, who I met in his record store when I first came to Geneva, and who introduced me around, had been killed in a robbery of his store. I learned about this when I stopped by the store and the new owners told me that two desperate-ass junkie thugs from the train station had robbed and shot him as was closing one night. It really hurt to hear that. He was not young when I met him, so these ass-hole thugs robbed and killed an elderly man. Damn shame.

There's no safe place from determined bad people. One must try to get the drop on them; and also move around cautiously. Did you encounter any other people from you past days in Geneva?
No, many people had moved away from Geneva. The Holdens I heard had moved to Palm Springs which was another home anyway. Betsy was living in France. Some hadn't been heard from in a while. I would say that this was Geneva closure for me. I saw Constance and Adriana, played a wonderful concert with The Art Ensemble of Chicago, and then left town. That was that.

Going back to '73 when Adriana got out of the hospital, where did you go when it became clear that neither Adriana nor Geneva was happening anymore?
I headed to Paris. Now this is a bit interesting, I think. Julio was living with a French-Italian lady, Beatrice Caracciolo. Adriana and I were instrumental in them becoming a pair. You see, one day while Adriana was in the *La Metairie*, I got a phone call about a terrible accident on the autobahn. The injured occupants of one of the cars were friends of Adriana: *Beatrice Caracciolo,*

and *Rick Heumann*. Rick died at the scene, and Beatrice had severe, but not life-threatening injuries. About two weeks after the accident Beatrice was transferred to a hospital in Paris. Of course, Adriana was unable to see Beatrice and console her during this difficult time. I spoke with Beatrice on the phone and told her I was sending my friend, Julio, to see if her, and that he would be checking regularly to see if she had any needs. This is how we did things. You come yourself, if possible, and if not, you sent an envoy. Well, Julio and Beatrice hit it off. They were together on and off for a lengthy period of time.

I gather meeting Beatrice was the beginning of another adventure!
Ha-ha! Oh yes! You know us! As some European bourgeois thinking goes, Beatrice was a woman of royalty, and noteworthy pedigree, which has nothing to do intelligence, spiritual balance, or experience. As it happened, Beatrice and Julio entered each other's lives when they both needed change, and the accompanying challenges. Beatrice was the daughter of Jean Caracciolo, a shareholder, and executive at *Banque Rothschild,* according to Beatrice. Beatrice came from wealth and was also a Principessa di Napoli.

Was Julio impressed?
I think he was initially a bit fascinated, but he was well aware of the shortcomings of those who flaunt titles, and the often-cruel history of European royals. It didn't take long for him put things in perspective, whereas Beatrice had a lot of learning to do about life outside of her culture. And let me tell you, sometimes that shit was too heavy to be around.
Oh, I can imagine. I'm sure their relationship was

turbulent with plenty of cultural misunderstandings.
You're right, and like I said, they were hard to be around sometimes. But we decided to go Corfu together and cool out. We all needed that. Me after Adriana. Beatrice, after the accident and death of her partner, Rick. And Julio, because being together with Beatrice was going to take some work. Corfu was a place where Julio and I had spent time, and we had many friends there; and for Beatrice, it would be her first trip to Greece.

We discussed your adventures in Corfu in your first book. All kinds of stuff happened. Coup d'état, the arrest of the Dixie White Girls, great love affairs. How was y'all's stay this time?
Well, it started off calmly enough. We contacted our friend, George Varthis, who rented us the house where Julio and Milly had lived before in the village of Parama. The house was bi-level. Julio and Beatrice occupied upstairs, and I resided downstairs. It was pleasant. I had my privacy, and they had theirs. We arrived in April of '73, so things were pretty quiet on the island except for the *St. Spyridon* festivities in Corfu Town when according to tradition, people drop plates from their windows onto the streets below. This is a festive time and one of many Greek Orthodox festivals.

As the weather warmed, more people started arriving on the island. More seasonal shops, bars, and restaurants opened, and the partying began. Soon, all of our old friends from Athens, London, and other places were there, and a whole new set people.

Were you actually able to cool-out as you had planned?

Well, yes, in the beginning. But, you know, we just went with the flow. Also, there were lots of other things going on in our lives outside of Greece. Beatrice had legal matters going on in France and Switzerland, so she and Julio made several trips back and forth over the course of the summer. I had family business in Canada, so I made a lengthy trip to Toronto, about a month.

I remember that. Wasn't that the first time you met your baby girl? And wasn't your sister recently married?
That's right. My daughter, Jessica, was born in 1972, and most regrettably, I wasn't able to get away from Geneva to go to Toronto. As I said in Book 1, this was during the time of great anger, distrust, and agitation between Linda and me. And as I've said, Geneva was complicated, and I had not yet extracted myself, let's say, responsibly.

You hadn't been in North America for a while, and now you're going back with an agenda full of family matters. Also, a lot has happened to you during the nearly four years since you left New York after winning a nice sum of money in a dice game. How were you feeling about all this?
I was excited. A lot had happened since leaving New York back in '69. On both sides of the ocean, many changes. Changes with my family, changes politically, changes in maturity, changes professionally, a whole lot. I was looking forward to being with my sister and our parents. I don't remember how many, but a few years had passed since we were all together. And I was really excited to see my daughter, Jessica.

Alright, Beau! Run with it!
I flew to Toronto via Athens. I checked into the King Edward Hotel on King Street in Toronto. From there I arranged rendezvouses with family and others. Others being the family of some people I had met in Greece. Seeing Jessica for the first time was knee weakening. I put her on my shoulders, and we walked around for a while.

Did she know who you were?
Well, she was told, but I don't think that had much meaning for her. I'm sure she felt something. As soon as I saw her, I was thinking of how to spend more time together. I gave some thought to moving to Toronto, sooner rather than later. Linda was not receptive to that idea. I can't say exactly what was going on in her life, but probably quite a bit of effort towards her modelling and acting career, and whatever that entailed. And so, it would a few years would pass before we all really got together. But it did happen, as a loving family that included Glenn, Linda's late husband, their child, Micah, and my children. All of us guided by the love of the Cosmics and our Ancestors.

It takes time to acquire balance and accept guidance. Continuing in Toronto…?
I met up with my parents, my sister, Margaret, and met her husband, John. Margaret and John met at Columbia University, they hit it off, and decided to marry. They seemed mismatched to me; however, who can speak to other people's feelings. A few years later, maybe around 1977, they were divorced. I've got the final decree amongst old papers. They didn't have children, and my sister never married again. I never got to be uncle Beau.

Did you like her husband?
No, I did not. He seemed a little misinformed to me, and somewhat patronizing. He thought he knew a whole lot more than he really did about Black people. There's a lot of presumption that goes with being from an influential family. A lot of what I call Euro-arrogance. In fact, the family doesn't have to be influential at all, that's some shit inherent to colonizing people and their offspring. And my sister found herself in an unfamiliar world. Years later, she acknowledged that incompatibility was the major factor that brought their relationship to an end. Sometimes it takes a while to find that out. The courts usually call it irreconcilable differences, and that usually sums it up no matter what those differences are.

More on your trip?
As I said, I was at the King Edward, and the bar there kept me entertained when I wasn't visiting the family or friends I had met in Greece. And then there was the *El Mocambo Nightclub* where I caught Chicago Bluesman, *Mighty Joe Young* one evening, and I also met a stunning young lady, Mary M. I don't know why, but nearly every woman I've ever met named Mary has been totally, and beautifully wild. As was the case with Mary M. And you know, she sure was fine!

Did you and Mary hang pretty tough?
Yes. When I wasn't dealing with family matters, Mary and I were hanging. In fact, she drove me around many areas of Toronto, and introduced me to some of her very nice young friends.

How old was Mary?
Well, truth be told, I don't really know. When I met her,

she said she was twenty. A few weeks later when I was back in Greece, she wrote in a letter that she was seventeen. Then when I wrote her back about that jailbait number, she said she was just joking, that she was really twenty. I met her in a nightclub. I didn't know drinking age laws in Toronto, I assumed that one had to be at least eighteen. She was just unhappy that I couldn't hang around Toronto a bit longer. We had fun though. While I was in Toronto, Bluesman and great friend, *Big Walter Horton* came to town and man did we have fun. One day Mary, Big Walter, some other folks, and I went to the Fort Erie Racetrack. Big Walter was *Mister Lucky*! He handicapped his ass off. He won most of the races and so did I because I bet with him: Daily Double, Trifecta, the regular stuff. So, racetrack day was a money party, and the evening was fun listening to Big Walter play at the *El Macomber*, and Mary and I dancing the night away.

Was Mary disappointed that you left?
Yes, she wanted to come back to Greece with me, but that would not have worked out because I had something going on with a couple of ladies on the Island. Also, I wasn't sure about my movements going into the fall. I started thinking about heading back to Canada, possibly Montréal. But I was mulling over many possibilities at that time. Being in Montréal would put me closer to my daughter, and closer to my family in Chicago. You know, time is moving quickly, and I'm thinking that my parents are moving along in years. So, Mary and I couldn't hang anymore after our Toronto fling. Like the Marys I have known before and after her, she possessed exquisite, unforgettable talents.

You were busy like a native Torontonian, how much

longer were you there?
Just a couple more weeks. The King Eddie was starting to take a toll on my finances, and Linda was not being cooperative with me as far as seeing my daughter was concerned. She thought she was punishing me, but in actuality, she was punishing our child. People are really fucked up in when it comes to breaking the chains of their past. If their childhood was a disaster, they angrily pass it on to their children. It's like they are saying, *'Why should you be happy, I wasn't?'* They make sure they repeat the same shit that happened to them by ruining every possibility for success. To give their children completeness seems not to be a consideration. Negative-ass, self-fulfilling prophecy. Projecting and inviting negative scenarios, I've known many like that.

Me too, as you know. It's like jealously over their own children's innocence, and unlimited potential. Anyway, did you move out of the King Eddie?
Yes, I had to. I had an acquaintance in Greece who was from Toronto. He arranged for me to stay in one of his family's properties for a few days. They were the Burns brothers who drank, gambled, drove fast cars, and complained that their father, a prominent Toronto attorney, didn't lavish them with stacks of cash for which they would not be held accountable. Sometimes they would get drunk and hope for, and often hypothetically plot his demise in rather disturbing detail. I thought, these is some spoiled-ass white boys who have been given so much by their dad: houses, cars, investment money for the futures market, and so on. But it was never enough because they had to make an effort to manage and demonstrate that they were capable. They were not. They were reckless and self-absorbed brats. I had to get away from around them. After five days, I

headed back to Corfu via Roma and Athens.

Have you closing thought about your trip?
After losing Adriana in Switzerland, and just trying to re-group from the intensity of the past year, it was great to checkout North America. To be in another rhythm. To hangout in a big city, you know, there was a sort of familiarity, but not comfort. I did pretty much resolve to spend more time there as I said, primarily for my parents and my daughter. But also, I was intrigued by all the money around. Those things eventually influenced my decision to eventually return to North America. These are thoughts I was having flying to Roma.

And back on Corfu?
I got some writing done. I played music at the *Club Med.* I started hanging with another Mary. By September, I was ready to head back to Paris, which is what Beatrice, Julio, and I did. I rented a house outside Paris near a village named *La Brosse.* From there we did a lot of gigs; Nancy, Strasbourg, Amsterdam, Delft, Brussels, Antwerp, London, and so many more. Still, the idea of North America was constantly on my mind. My thoughts took the form of unfinished business. There were things I had to find out. Things that I needed clarity about; political, social injustice, America's systemic racism. I needed to re-bond with my family. To learn more from my mother and father, and other elders. You know, I left the crib initially at seventeen, partially in a huff, and for good at eighteen. That goes with age. Now, at this time, I'm twenty-four and had been in Europe four and a half years and been on the move for seven years. I decided to revisit the U.S. near the end of December '73. Just like that! That's the way to work it. Think it, then act.

**21 September 2019
Le Château Frontenac
Terrasse Dufferin
Québec City, Québec**

On Revisiting the United States

LaBosse, here we are, again. This is like revisiting a dream, walking with you here. How many times have we been here and over the past fifty years and pondered, planned, reminisced, and have been enthralled by the beauty of this place as far as the eye can see. Just watching the St. Lawrence being navigated by ships, and the ferry to Levis, all of this brings back incredibly vivid memories of my youth, and the times we've spent here with friends. Anyway, back to my story.

And so you decided to revisit the US. How was that journey, and was there a bit of culture shock?
I flew to Chicago after hanging in London for a few days. And yes, there was manageable culture shock briefly; and occasionally, I regretted the move but convinced myself to stay the course. It was great seeing my parents again after Toronto which was only about six months previous. They had moved since I was last there. They were living at 72nd and Coles Avenue in South Shore, when I left home, we lived at 69th and Clyde Avenue in the same neighbourhood. I hadn't been on the neighbourhood in Chicago since I was about eighteen. Not much had changed. People on the scene were older. There were stories about who got shot, what idiot robbed the pool room, and other stories. Not much had changed. All and all pretty damn boring.

I gather your visit was brief?
Yes, brief indeed. But even though the old neighbourhood was boring, it was pleasant being around some of the things I grew up with that my parents had brought to their new apartment. My mom kept certain books, toys, documents, pieces of furniture, which gave my parents great memories of our family life. I am very appreciative for what my sister and I experienced growing up. So, yea, nostalgia! But the hood, the cats, the vibe; that shit was not happening.

After about a week I decided to head to San Francisco where I had a few contacts. And also, I had visited San Francisco with my family as a youngster, and as a teenager. I was around sixteen but looking much older, so I managed to have a couple of adventures.

I recall you telling me about a Strip Club.
Well, I had travelled to San Francisco with my mother and sister. Let's see, this was 1965, I was sixteen. We were staying with my Dad's sister, Viola, and her husband Al; they helped me convince my mother that it was safe for me to go out alone at night. When I think back, I know my mother must have been worried sick. Anyway, I got to go out by myself, so I went straight to the North Beach naked houses. I forget the names of some of them. I remember the Condor where Carol Doda performed. Anyway, I met a musician, nice brother, in one of them joints, and after a while, we decided to go to the Trident in Sausalito, across the Golden Gate, where George Duke was playing, and I sat in with him on harmonica. Interestingly, many years later, around 2006, I saw him again at *Espoo Jazz Festival in Finland,* where I was the Emcee. He fondly and vividly remembered our Sausalito encounter. George is now an Ancestor!

Praises! Beautiful person!

I've digressed a bit, but I like that San Francisco story. As I was saying, I had some connections. There was Aunt Viola and Al, Cousin Jimmie Lee and her husband, Jim. Milly Hurlimann was there, she introduced my friend, Julio Finn and me to Corfu, Greece back in 1971 when we were all living in Paris. And there was Julio's brother, Jerome Arnold, who was a Blues bass player originally from Chicago. He had worked with *Howling Wolf, Johnny Twist, The Paul Butterfield Blues Band,* and many others. When I got to San Francisco he was leading his own group, *The Jerome Arnold Blues Band.*

You had it going on. Surely, it didn't take you too long to establish your presence on the scene.
Not at all. When I got there, I stayed with Jerome at his crib at 112 Lundys Lane in the Mission District. I played a few gigs with his band, but still, that wasn't making any money. I had to find a way to make money that was fun, exciting, and a new experience. I mean, I hadn't been in the United States for nearly five years, and I had been on the road since 1966, except for a few months in '67 preparing for departure. I was unknown musically in San Francisco. Some Jazz fans, a few musicians and others knew about my recordings with Archie Shepp, and the Art Ensemble of Chicago, but San Francisco is a long way from Paris, with its own diverse and vibrant culture, art cliques, and distinct rhythm. I didn't take me long to get into the groove!

Now I know it didn't take you long to hook up with a lady or two, or three, right?
Actually, I was a bit out of step with American women. One has to learn the mores if you will. A compliment to

a lady in France could very well be an insult to a lady from Oakland, or they may be flattered. But I did make some headway. I'll tell you more later. There's another thing that took some getting used to, and that's daily racism all up in your face. Yes, for sure there is serious racism in colonizing Europe mentality, it's just presented with less underlying hate, suspicion, and discrimination. Also, in Europe a Black musician was novel, an exception, a cultural icon. The French have a huge Jazz history and love for Black musicians going back to WW1 that has been well documented. As you know, many Black artists throughout the African diaspora have been welcomed in European countries like France, Denmark, Switzerland, and more. The relationship with people who like what you do, is very different from people who hate because you are Black or have colour no matter what you do. That's part of the soullessness of the United States. Just look around, and maybe duck!

Where you able to find a suitable way to earn some money?
Yes. One day I was reading the *Want Ads* in the *San Francisco Chronicle* and saw a job listing for a door-to-door salesperson to sell colour portraits.

Selling in a way has always been your thing. Selling ideas, books, yourself. You are not shy, and you know how to listen.
Ha-ha! Tell it! This was really a fun experience for me, and I made a good living as soon as learned the ropes of the colour portrait, family photo business. For starters, I interviewed with Stevie Benson, the owner of *Westlake Studio of Color*, which was located in an older building at Third and Mission in San Francisco. Our initial chat was pretty good. This was totally new territory

for me, convincing a white man that I could do the job. Fortunately, I had a few references from my younger days working in banks and grocery stores back in Chicago that seemed to impress him. But the crews he assembled to go do-to-door in the San Francisco suburbs were hardly individuals with sterling credentials. They were mostly older ladies and gentlemen who were struggling to make ends meet. A number of them lived in flophouses in the *Tenderloin District.* Some were retired and just wanted something to do. And then me, I was trying to make a couple of bucks, and experience some aspects of America unknown to me.

I'm seeing that a crew was actually quite diverse and consisted of people outside of the norm.
Exactly. Let me break it down for you, the portrait business. First, the concept. People like pictures of their children at all ages as they grow up. Generally, children grow fast, and doting parents and grandparents want constant updates on the children's progress and changes. Therefore, on most any house door you knock on where there are kids, you have a very good chance of making a sale. Even if they say they had pictures taken recently, they were easy to convince that more are needed especially since what we are offering was unparalleled professional photography at a price that beat Sears or other department store photo studios. Next, the crews. The crews of three or more people depending on the capacity of the car would meet in mornings or get picked up by the crew chief around 9:00A.M. just after rush hour. Part of the Crew Chiefs job was to pick a neighbourhood to be worked that day, and as you know, the Bay Area is huge. I started with a crew that had been working the East Bay. They had hit Walnut Creek, Livermore, Pleasanton, Danville, and other

towns. My first day was in a subdivision in Newark. Crew members were assigned to work about three residential streets. If we started at 10:30, we'd be done around 2:30, and that would leave plenty of time to get back to San Francisco before the evening rush.

How did that first day go?
It was very interesting for a number of reasons. As a beginner the crew chief sent someone along with me. I was accompanied by a guy named Imro, who was originally from Czechoslovakia, now the Czech Republic. Imro was one of those unfortunate immigrants that was well educated in his homeland, but his degrees were unacceptable in the United States academic system. He had been married to an American woman, but they had been divorced for quite some time. At this time, he was in his sixties in living in a tiny room in the *Tenderloin*. Imro was a good companion. He was well travelled and a pleasure to be with. Imro showed me the ropes. There wasn't much, mostly protocol relating to things like, after you ring a doorbell be sure to stand back, and never go in a house even the parents yell it's okay if a child answered the door. Be sure to be invited in directly by an adult, which was one of the most important rules.

How did a presentation work? I'm sure that you improvised.
Ring the bell or knock. If they open the door without asking who it is be sure to be several feet back. If they ask who is there, announce loudly, but politely, 'Hi, I'm with Westlake Studio of Color, and I have a special offer for baby and family portraits. Then stand back. I'd say 90 percent of the time people would listen. During the week it was usually moms at home who were interested. On weekends, dads maybe home, and some-

times they were a bit more difficult to engage. The key is to establish a good vibe right from the beginning. That's why it's important to have your sample picture out at all times. When they open the door or look through a peep hole, they see a baby picture, or family grouping, and your solicitor's badge issued by the local police, if required.

Now you, being a Black man of over six feet tall, and carrying 275 pounds of weight, surely the immediate reaction by some white people must have been intimidation.
Certainly, some people were, but generally, they were not. You see, this was happening during a period when America was going through another transition. These were probably the last days of what had been easily one hundred-fifty years of peddler culture. That was part of the culture of capitalism, to be able to buy things from the convenience of home. There were people selling reclining chairs, kitchen ware and utensils, shoes, religion, encyclopaedias, Girl Scout Cookies, and lord knows what else. One could enrol in a Dale Carnegie sales course from the back of a comic book. People were used to salespeople in housing tracts and subdivisions. Also, it wasn't that a Black person would do anything to a white family, too many witnesses, and the police know you're around. I think being a door-to-door salesperson today, no matter the skin colour, would be ill-advised. Too dangerous for all parties concerned. It's another bit of history replaced by politician inspired fear, racial profiling, and technology. Nowadays, here in Kansas City, and all across the United States people of colour are being killed by the police, and others just being in their own neighbourhoods. I mean these motherfucking police is killing Black people in they own cribs, just

trying to relax, sleep, or prepare a meal. And you have politicians, like Trump and many of his lackeys, who encourage it by not denouncing it.

It's strange, conditioning. When you were knocking on doors, even if people were racist, they were conditioned to accept your presence as non-threatening, and quite possibly, vital to their needs.
Exactly, and they knew that a salesperson of colour was an agent for some white business. So generally, people were pretty cool.

How did things go after your training?
I ain't bragging, but being a musician and entertainer, and having learned how to work crowds, and also having learned how to sell myself, I was armed with very useful assets. And my training was only two days. On the second day I asked Irmo my trainer if we could split up, meaning that he would work one side of the street, and I would work the other. He agreed. We started. I started my cruise looking for yards that showed signs of children, like bikes and toys in the front yard, and cars in the driveway. I found selling appointments to be quite easy because, as I said, people love pictures of their kids. And the deal was cheap. The offer was an 8 x 10 photo for ninety-nine cents, plus $1.00 for every extra person in the photo. A family of four was $3.99. The salesperson got to keep that money. That's how we got paid. The customer got a certificate with a tentative date and time for the photographer to come and shoot the photos. On a good day, which for me was typical, I made an average of $80.00, which was shocking to other members of the crew.

What was your formula?

Okay, typically the salesperson would concentrate on the household they we selling to, then book the photographer at the earliest possible date. My approach was to suggest that they make the photo shoot a larger family gathering. I suggested to set an appointment far enough out so that grandparents and maybe other relatives could be in the photo. Many were pleased with that suggestion, so a portrait of four became possibly a portrait of six or eight. Then the people were so please with my suggestion and willingness to suggest outfits, etc. If they were going to give me a ten- or twenty-dollar bill for payment, they just let it change ride. It all adds up. By 2 or 2:30, quitting time, I had made my money. I ain't bragging, or putting the others down, they just weren't skilled enough to deviate from the normal presentation. Now on that first day alone with Imro working the other side of the street, I made $70.00, the crew was astonished. Imro made $40.00. At that time making $70.00 for around four hours work was darn good.

Did your early success impress your crew chief and the studio owner?
It did. And I knew I was headed for a larger role in the portrait business. Here's the rest of the order in the business, and why it worked so well. It's all about real communication. Real people skills, not robo-call, cell phone babble, by inexperienced lead burners. After the appointment was made, a skilled photographer came to the home to take the pictures. Typically, the photo was shot in front of a sky-blue background that is still quite popular today. The photographer would take many shots and poses, making sure that there were cute pictures of all the kids, grandparents, parents, in every combination. The photographer got paid around $20.00 per client, and usually had ten to fifteen sessions per

run. Next comes the money maker. The proof passer. A good proof passer tries to make up to ten appointments a day, and strongly suggests to the clients that family members be there to look at the photos. The proofs to be viewed were colour slides, sometimes called transparencies, which are 2x2 inches, depending on manufacturer. The slides are viewed on a small hand-held lighted magnifier or projected onto a large screen. It's certainly possible to show proofs on a small screen, and the client may get excited about the pictures. But when you show up with a screen and projector, if the client don't have it, that's going to make it easier to close a deal.

Beau, tell us about the deal.
Oh yeah. Got a little ahead of myself. Remember when the initial salesperson made the sale, the client got and 8x10 colour photo at a discounted price. Now, when the proof passer went around, they asked the people to pick the photo they want for the special price. When that's done the proof passer, or salesperson really, proposes various packages that include more poses and different sizes. Some clients are ready for this, some seem surprised, and some, not many, take their special offer and escort your ass to the door wile telling you that 'you ain't going to hustle me.' Happens!

Photo packages ranged in price from around $19.95 to beyond $100.00. for the cheaper price one probably got 2 5x7's and 6 wallet sizes. Not much. Then there was something with a ridiculous title like the 'Grand Ma Special' for $59.95, that may have consisted of two 8x10s, six 5x7s, and 12 wallet sizes. Kick it up a notch to maybe the Graduation or Engagement Special for $79.95: one 11 x 14, four 8x10s, twelve 5 x 7s, and six wallet sizes. Hey! One heck of a deal! Beyond this a good proof passer just created deals. You know, worked with the family budget to create what they wanted. Proof passers made a 25 percent commission. On an $80.00 sale, that's $20.00. The wholesale price for the package is around $10.00. That leaves $50.00. The photographer got $20.00, that leaves $30.00 profit for the company. Now Westlake ran five crews a day in all directions out of San Francisco. They went north to Marin County and beyond, south on the Peninsula, the East Bay, the Sunset and Richmond districts of San Francisco.

If every day you had twenty proof passers working averaging $30.00 in profit x 10 times daily, that's a profit of $6,000 per day. A good proof passer, like I came to be, made between $150 and $200 dollars an outing. On terrible days Westlake made $1500-$3000.00. And Benson, the owner, he was living quite lavishly in Burlingame, a fairly wealthy suburb south of San Francisco.

Not bad at all, and not hard work.
No, it was mostly enjoyable. And I realize that $150-$200 a day isn't much in today's world. You probably couldn't rent the space under someone's kitchen sink in San Francisco for that tiny money. But back then I was living well. Not extravagant, but well enough.

How long did selling photographs keep your attention?
About a year. But in the last few months it was done on a need to do basis, and not with Westlake, but my own company.
Why did you leave Westlake? Like I can't guess!

Money. Once I saw the breakdown of expenses and profits, I really had no choice. So, one of the photographers, Patrick 'Straight out of Ireland' Mahoney, and I decided to break off from Westlake and start our own company. We called it *Photographe Intenationale.* And we also rented an apartment in San Bruno, in a complex called *Crystal Springs Terrace*, which was our home, office and studio. But the photos we took there were mostly of friends. Anyway, we had a two-man operation. Pat and I would both book appointments as door-to-door salesmen. Then Pat would take the photos, and afterwards I would make the sales. No middleman. And to give you an idea about the mark-up, the 8" x 10" matted photo that Westlake sold for $20.00, cost under $2.00 to make. Basically, a $59.95 'Grandma Special' with various sizes of photos cost about $10.00. So, Pat and I were doing about forty shoots a week. Not everybody bought, some just wanted the freebie we offered at initial contact with the customer. However, if we sold thirty packages averaging around sixty bucks each, we made around $650 each a week after expenses. And we only worked three or four days a week, and not all day. Then there were some weeks we decided to really crank out the sales. That would consist of call-backs, price breaks, and working five or six days straight. When we did that, we took in around $3000 in profits to split. We may have done that that twice. Too exhausting. San Francisco in 1975 was not expensive. We were living well.

The door-to-door business was part of your reintroduction into living in America, and it seems to me that doing that business gave you an experience that many people will never have. You used your entertainer skills, and you were able to convince

buyers of the benefits of what you were selling. What was your next move after the photography business?
There was a lot going on socially and musically. I started playing more with the *Jerome Arnold Blues Band.* I was meeting people at gigs and doing a lot of hanging out with an old friend from Paris and Corfu, Milly. Milly had a friend who was a partner in *The Great American Music Hall,* which had live performances nightly of nearly every type of popular music. That scene became a regular place to hang. There was another circle of musicians that were associated with a band called *Stroke.* I met the trumpet player, *Earl Coleman,* through *Sam Stafford*, the excellent guitarist in Jerome's band.

Let me digress for a moment. Jerome's band had two players that went on to become master instrument makers and teachers: drummer, David Kindred, now in North Carolina; and Sam Stafford, now in Tennessee.

Are you in touch with them?
With David, but not Sam. However, David keeps me posted about Sam's excellence as a luthier. Anyway, Sam introducing me to Earl Coleman ending up having a major impact on my life that is still resounding beautifully.

This sounds pretty intriguing, let it roll!
Okay, here we go. Sam and Earl were roommates over on Bosworth St., and I used to visit frequently. One day Earl suggested that I come hear the R & B band he had recently joined, *Stroke.* And he said that the lead singer, Dan, had a following of fine ladies. So, I went over to a club in Alameda, that I can't recall the name of, but It

was a live music hotspot in the East Bay. Dan had a girlfriend, Caroline. The night that I went to the club, Caroline had come with her older sister, Rose. Rose and I locked eyes from the jump. Seemed like magical invisible beings were pushing us closer and closer together. We went our separate ways that evening but got in touch the next day. We met for lunch, then she came by my house where we had a lovely evening. You know how things can just seem right?

Oh yes. I remember I couldn't get you off the phone about Rose. I told you not to kill your phone calling me for an hour at a time in Paris. Long distance calls back then were seriously expensive.
Well, it's great that it all worked out. So, after about a month of being inseparable, we decided to give living together a try.

Rose had family and friends in the area, right?
Yes. Rose's mother, sister, and brother lived in a nice home in Alameda. Rose convinced her mom to invite me over for Sunday dinner, which was a Swisher family tradition. I got along well with them; however, her mom, GeorgiaB, was sceptical because of my travels. I was not the ideal compliant young Black man she thought I should be. But in time we worked through all of that and became friends. The Swisher's were from the Houston, Texas area, and let me tell you, GeorgiaB cooked up some outrageously delicious Tex-Mex-African cuisine. The enchiladas, burritos, salads, chili. Man, I have never tasted anything from that region or many others that can come close to GeorgiaB's cooking!

How did the other family members feel about you?
Rose had three teenage children, two sons, Jacob, and

Bill Jr, the eldest; and a daughter, Karen, who was the youngest. I didn't meet Rose's children for a few weeks after she and I got together, they were with their dad in Seattle. And also, Rose needed to find a house because up until shortly before I met her, she had been living in the Boston area, where she and her family had lived previously. How they felt about me was not yet established.

So, she came to the Bay Area because of family. I take it that her cross-country move was because of a big change in her life.
Correct. She was recently divorced and decided to be closer to her family. And so, we went about the business of trying to find a house that would be suitable for five people. We knew that my presence may not be accepted by her children, or child support and alimony paying ex.

We found a house in the Oakland Hills just off Skyline Drive. The kids came shortly thereafter, and then began the intricate and delicate process of introducing me. In fact, I was not there when the children first arrived. That would have been too much, too soon. I stayed in San Francisco for about ten days after the children came. Rose invited me for dinner. I said no, let's get a list of what everybody would like to have, and I'll have the food delivered. That worked out well because she really didn't have much by way of kitchenware etc. All of her things were being brought by movers across country, and that was still two or three weeks from actually happening.

How did the first meeting go? Did the kids seem to like you?

Her sons and I really hit it off well. Her daughter was a bit more reserved. She was also the youngest and had a very strong attachment to her dad, which I can certainly appreciate. Rose told her children that we had been dating and that we were becoming more and more serious, and were thinking about me moving in. The boys initial reaction was very positive, whereas Karen had no reaction. Eventually, I did move in, and Karen chose to live with her dad, and I think that was a good decision because he gave her the overall protection and parenting that she wanted and needed. We became a house of four people with visits by Karen from time-to-time. And with each visit she was more comfortable.

What month is this now?
This is May of 1974.

I'm trying to keep your movements straight in my head. Exactly one year prior, where were you?
I was in Corfu, Greece; followed by Toronto; then LaBroose, France; then London; then Chicago for a few, and then what we've been talking about, my early days in San Francisco. Quite a year! I can't imagine it any other way.

Me neither. Now, you are 'Suburban Man' living in the Oakland Hills. Did the children attend school in the area?
They attended Skyline High School, and we shopped at the Skyline Market. We were a family of Black Skyliners, which was met with some resentment by a couple of neighbours. One who told me quite bluntly that one of his reasons for moving to Skyline was to get away from 'people like us.'

To which you responded?
Ha-ha! I told him that we had moved there specifically to annoy people like him, and that I was delighted that we were having success. He then got into his grey 1972 Oldsmobile Delta 88 and drove off.

This is a major change, you were accustomed to scenery, rhythm, people, international vibe, languages. I mean hearing only California English. Good lord! How did you adjust? In San Francisco you have an international vibe, Latin and Asian vibes, and there is tourism, and the city has character. But man, I'm trying to imagine you in the Oakland Hills at that time in your life.
It wasn't as insular as Kansas City, that's for certain. Let me try to give a you picture of what was going on. First, I must admit that I was fatigued. I had been on the move since 1966, except for a few months in Chicago, which I left on my mom's birthday, December 29, 1967. I had been on the move since then, seven years that saw me grow from a teenager to a man. From playing music in mining camps and on street corners, to working and recording with some of the greatest musicians of all time. I'd gone from living in a twenty-dollar a week room in Québec City to having a house account at the Hotel Sainte James et d'Albany on the rue du Rivoli in Paris. I've damn near walked from Boston to Montréal, and I've been flown on a private jet to Tangier. Yes, slightly fatigued, but not as an encumbrance. It was more about having some time to reflect. Some time to have yet another kind of experience, which is what was happening with Rose and her children, and with her mom and her siblings. I was welcomed into a large Black family that had numerous components, and numerous les-

sons for me to learn. And I had much to share with them. I kind of immersed myself in drab suburbia. Mind you, I did have activities and interest that took me to San Francisco from time-to-time, like hanging out at the Music Hall and seeing some of my relatives on my father's side. He had a sister. Viola, who lived on Bayshore near Silver, and my dad had a niece, his brother's child, who lived at the top of Pine. Believe me, those houses are mega bucks today. I occasionally visit my relatives and fascinate them with stories about by travel, fun, and some risky situations that left them in awe. And so for me the Skyline residence was a place of repose, not isolation.

What were some of your activities with Rose and family during this period?
Rose and I decided to start going to *Bay Meadows Racetrack,* at the suggestion of an old family friend of hers whose name escapes me. Also, I had gone to a few races in the recent past during my trip to Toronto, at *Fort Erie Racetrack.* I lucked out and won a few dollars along with my betting partner, Bluesman, *Big Walter Horton.*

I've never known you to be much of a gambler, but I do recall you winning decent amounts of money from time-to-time, especially when you needed it.
That's right. I had some money woes in the south of France, and the *Casino de Monte Carlo* came through nicely, as I won a few thousand Francs playing Boule. The same thing happened once at the *Casino de Cassis near Marseille.* And back when I was twenty, I got into a pretty intense crab game in a hotel room in New York that netted me a couple of grand. These were all somewhat urgent situations, and the Cosmics lit my

way.

How was your luck with the horses?
I think luck is the right word. However, there may be some skill involved if one looks at statistics, like the horses record on grass or dirt track. The horses bloodline. The performance record of the jockey. How do each perform in certain weather conditions. Who is the trainer, and the trainer's record. All of this information is available in the *Daily Racing Forum*. And after reading all of the statistics, one just tries to make a good guess. I usually leaned toward the Jockey's performance. *Laffit Pincay, Jr.,* and *Sandy Hawley* are two that come to mind. I made money with both of them. Then there is playing your hunch, going with the horses name, or birthdate. All of these things make gambling what it is, a gamble. Nothing is certain in a horserace, gaming table, or any other gambling platform.

For Rose and me it was not only betting and handicapping, but it was also the ambience of the Turf Club. We would have lunch, chat with people, watch people, have a few drinks, and generally have a good time. I remember a great handicapper named Joey. He liked to be called Pal Joey, like from the film. He liked that. He was from Salerno, Italy, and had been living in the States for many years. The three of us having lunch became a regular thing. Pal Joey knew horses; he knew the game. About eighty percent of his recommendations worked. Sometimes not for much. He taught to me to go with 'Win, Place, Show' always on the favourites, and back up my Exacta bets the same way. Well. Sometimes you could lose it all, and sometimes, you could win a lot. Pal Joey's advice worked often enough to keep us in the game.

I know you like fun and people. What else was going on when you decided to sortie?
Here's another fun thing Rose and I got into. As I said earlier, she was having all of her belongings shipped from Boston. When her things arrived, and she started going through everything, she realized that there was so much that neither she nor her children wanted to keep. This massive moving van was filled to the brim, we could barely get everything in the house and garage. And so, we started having garage sales on Saturdays and Sundays. This went on for about a month. During this time some interesting people came by the house because we had advertised in the local paper that we had Jazz and Blues records to sell. This of course attracted buyers with that particular interest. Talk small world, a piano player, *Mark Naftilin,* saw our ad and came over from San Rafael to check out the collection. Mark was the piano player in the original *Paul Butterfield Blues Band*, that my friend Jerome Arnold was in at the same time. I hadn't seen Mark since 1967. Mark and I started hanging out a bit, and as it turned out, Mark knew my dear friend Milly Hurlimann. Another customer was Yuri C., who was a diplomat at the Russian Consulate in San Francisco. Yuri was a big Jazz and Blues fan, so we became friends. What followed were dinner parties, hanging out at night clubs, and so on. And so, LaBosse, that suburban rather nondescript home at 28 Knoll Ridge Way, became a catalyst for all kinds of fun, as well as being a quiet family residence where I could periodically isolate.

The more you speak, I get the feeling that this situation is precisely what you needed at that time in your life.

It was. But like I said, I was fatigued. Being with Rose and family gave me the best of many possibilities. I had family. I had fun with new acquaintances. I had a pleasant place to write and think as the back of the house was situated at the edge of the Redwood forest. And Rose was a beautiful and intelligent woman who fulfilled all of my desires and more, and she said the same thing about me. And so, this was a special period in our lives.

Where you playing music at all during this period?
I got a big surprise one day. I remembered that *Marva Broome,* a singer I knew in Paris, said that she was from Oakland. Let me say this quickly: Oakland has always been home to many great artists including *Tower of Power, Pointer Sisters, M.C. Hammer, Edwin Hawkins* and many, many more. Now back to Marva. I decided to see if I could find any Broome's in the White Pages telephone directory. I found a couple of Broome's, but no one with the first name Marva. I called the first Broome, and when the party answered, I identified myself, then asked if a Marva lived there? 'This is Marva.,' Then silence. Then she shouted, 'Childe! I had to catch my breath. Chicago Beau!' We couldn't believe that we were speaking with each other, in Oakland.

Was catching up with Marva motivation for you to play music?
Yes, it was because she was singing with a piano player named Maurice, as part of a duo. So, I went to some of their gigs from time-to- time and sat in. Also, Jerome Arnold's band had dissolved, so that wasn't happening anymore. Playing with Marva and Maurice was perfect, and sometimes they had a full rhythm section.

Things seem to be really balanced. This is a good place to be. Did it continue?
Yes. These recent events like the garage sales, hooking-up with Marva, and the racetrack took place within three or four months of us moving into the house. Rose and I also had a stand at the *San Jose Flea Market.* We did that a few times, and really met some interesting people, like collectors of all kinds of items from baseball cards to yo-yos. An amazing place, that market.

Around September, I was introduced to Willie Johnson, a songwriter and guitarist who had spent some time playing with *The Whispers R & B group. The Whispers* are still going, since the early 1960s. Willie was a fine guitarist and arranger. And so after a while I decided to put a band together and start rehearsals. The house was perfect because we had a really large living room that we never used. And so it commenced, slowly easing back into playing music, and on a scene where I was totally unknown. Willie and I formed the Nasty Band, and I can't remember who all was in the band, but personnel changed a lot even before our first gig. It was crazy. Musicians would show up at our house at rehearsals uninvited. People wanted to play music. The word was out that there was a new band forming, and people just came. That was really something!

And now after months of quiet contemplation and reflection, you having rehearsals in your living room. Quite a change. What did Rose and the rest of the family think about that?
They liked the idea right away. And thinking back, I think I held only three rehearsals, which after taking care of business, escalated into a mild party. All good though, everyone was very respectful of our home. On the other

hand, the neighbours who told me that he moved to Skyline to get away from people like us, complained by dropping off a nasty, racist letter complaining about noise and people coming and going, in our mailbox.

Did you respond?
We wanted to brighten the old grouch's day, so we neatly packaged a *Hustler Magazine,* and other more graphic publications, and put them in his mailbox. Never heard another peep from him.

Ha-ha! Maybe that helped him restore or discover a bit of zest in his marriage. Did the band start doing gigs?
Yes, we did. Rose and I bought a large Ford Econoline van, and had it customized to accommodate four musicians, three amps, and a drum set. It was really comfortable. The first gig was at *Orphans* in San Francisco, then way up on the Russian River in a town called Monte Rio at a club called *The Pink Elephant.*

I had a surprise at that gig because Jerome Arnold showed up. I didn't know it, but he had moved to Monte Rio with his new girlfriend. That was a great surprise, and we all had a great time. But actually, there were not many gigs around that paid well. I had the idea to do fund raising gigs for charity. Certain organizations would pay you more for time and travel expenses than you would make in a club playing three or four sets. And so, we played at fund raisers for *Cystic Fibrosis* and other charities. The gigs had a concert and party format with guest speakers, raffles, awards, etc.; and the money was very good.

Seems like that was a good plan, especially if you

were unknown to club owners and the locals.
I've always had an aversion to competing with other bands for club work, and the pettiness that sometimes is part of playing locally. Musicians have to do a lot to survive, the cats in the band were playing with other bands as well, and I certainly couldn't complain about that. And so, we did a few gigs here and there, but nothing like I was used to when I was playing in Europe. But we had fun, and I got to meet some really fine people.

You certainly had a lot going on. Were you able to continue to rest and regenerate?
Absolutely. Another new experience for me was that that I became a quasi-father figure for Rose's sons. When I met Rose I told her I was thirty years old, which would have made her six years older than me, which I thought would acceptable. I was right. I don't think she would have believed my real age of twenty-five anyway with all of the experiences I had.

Quick digression: *Rose came to visit me in Rome in 2000. I was 51 years old; she was 64. I was only at this time she became aware of my true age. She was totally surprised; however, as we reflected back on our times together, she agreed that the lie was better. And her family, unbeknownst to me, were concerned that she was seeing someone younger who was a vagabond, by their standards.*

So, I had experienced a lot, and had a lot to share with her sons, and to teach them. Jacob, the younger son, and I became great friends, and still are today. I'm happy to say that I was truly a positive influence on those young men. Jacob is a fine artists and graphic designer, and he has been a part of several of my projects over the years. Bill, the older brother, was wired quite differently than his brother, and I don't mean that in a negative way. I convinced Jacob to travel internationally, which he still does. And he is a family man with three children, living a blessed life. And, he is a master Tuba player!

You are presenting an extremely harmonious period, were their ever any major snags in that harmony?
I wouldn't call them major, or anything that couldn't be dealt with. There was criticism from Rose's mother after a few drinks. The more I spoke about my life and travels, the more suspect GeorgiaB would become. Her perception of what a young man should be doing in life was worlds apart from what I had been doing. Her ideas were typical: get a job, keep it, retire, and die. And occasionally in that forty-or-fifty-year period, take a few vacations; and if to visit family somewhere, sit around drinking, and rehashing old arguments.

On some holidays that are meant to be celebratory, we'd all head over to GeorgiaB's, and depending who was around, and the amount of booze, there may, or may not be arguments and disagreements, some of which had been going on amongst them for decades. I found this to be mostly amusing, and Bill and Jacob didn't take the rants and accusations seriously either. I would say that our harmony was not interrupted, because we didn't consider it to be. And so, on Skyline we had wonderful family vibes, interesting acquaintances, a bit of commerce, a great mini-wine cellar, music, nature, and a *Boxer* named *Patches*. Also, Rose got me into playing tennis, which I played rather well until health issues got to me in 2003 in Portugal.

Selected Photographs and Mementos

THE JOHN MARSHALL LAW SCHOOL

315 SOUTH PLYMOUTH COURT CHICAGO, ILLINOIS 60604
Telephone: 312-427-2737   Facsimile: 312-427-8307

OFFICE OF THE DEAN

December 16, 1996

Mr. Lincoln Beauchamp
58020 Bocchecagiano
Podere Potenziano
Italy

Dear Mr. Beauchamp:

I was pleased to be able to talk with you before you left for Italy. I look forward to visiting with you when you return.

As we discussed, the School is most interested in looking at the notes and memorabilia of your father regarding The John Marshall Law School.

My best wishes to you for a Happy Holiday and a healthy and prosperous New Year.

Sincerely,

Robert Gilbert Johnston
Dean

RGJ:dd

February 18, 1988

Mr. Lincoln Beauchamp
Editor and Publisher
Literati Chicago
5 N. Wabash Avenue
Chicago, IL 60602

Dear Mr. Beauchamp:

On behalf of the Board, Maestro Freeman and the staff, I would like to thank you for coverage given to the Chicago Sinfonietta.

Inclusion in your debut issue of Literati Chicago not only gives us excellent exposure, but it breeds a kinship between two art forms which we hope will last.

Congratulations and much continued success to Literati Chicago. The debut issue was excellent and we look forward to the next.

Again, my many thanks to you and Literati Chicago.

With best regards,

Karen Wojcik
Public Relations Coordinator

cc Maureen Kaucher, General Manager

Rosary College • 7900 West Division Street • River Forest, Illinois 60305 • 312/366-1062
Paul Freeman, music director • Maureen F. Kaucher, general manager

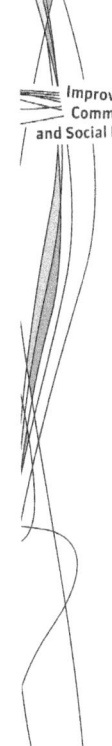

Improvisation,
Community,
and Social Practice

Lincoln Beauchamp
3849 Woodside Ave, 2nd Floor
Brookfield, IL
60513
USA

October 12, 2010

Dear Lincoln,

I am writing to send a sincere and more formal thank you for your contribution to the 2010 Guelph Jazz Festival Colloquium, "Improvising Bodies". Your engaging and insightful presentation played a significant role in contributing to the success of our event.

This year's colloquium initiated and fostered a variety of provocative discussions regarding the ways in which improvisation and the body intersect. The presentations, workshops, and discussions that took place over the course of this 3-day colloquium fully engaged our audience and brought about new ways of understanding the improvising body. We sincerely hope that the stimulating dialogue that came out of this year's colloquium will further inspire discussion around the possibilities of improvised music and its relation to the body.

I encourage you to consider contributing your work to *Critical Studies in Improvisation / Études critiques en improvisation*, our peer-reviewed journal (www.criticalimprov.com). We accept submissions on an ongoing basis for our general issues.

Again, I thank you for your contributions to this year's Guelph Jazz Festival Colloquium. We very much appreciate the time and effort you put into making this year's colloquium so successful, and I hope to see you at future colloquia.

Best wishes,

Ajay Heble
Professor, School of English and Theatre Studies, University of Guelph
Artistic Director, The Guelph Jazz Festival and Colloquium
Project Director, Improvisation, Community, and Social Practice

Fachhochschule Mannheim
Hochschule für Sozialwesen

Landesmuseum für
Technik und Arbeit Mannheim

Gastvortrag zum Thema

Black Music As Oral Culture

Referent

Lincoln Beauchamp
"Chicago Beau"
Montreal
Canada

Mittwoch, 15. Mai 1996

18.00 Uhr

Nach dem Vortrag beginnt das AStA-Fest mit dem angekündigten Konzert

Ort: Landesmuseum für Technik und Arbeit

Das Landesmuseum für Technik und Arbeit ist mit der Straßenbahnlinie 6 erreichbar
Haltestelle Landesmuseum

SHADES OF BLUES:

A Conversation on the Classic Works of August Wilson and Lonne Elder III from a Blues (Music) Perspective

Saturday, November 3, 2012 from 4-6pm
The Reva and David Logan Center for the Arts
915 E. 60th Street @ Drexel Blvd., Room 801

Dr. Mikell Pinkney   Dr. Ken Warren   Lincoln Beauchamp, Jr.

eta Creative Arts Foundation, in collaboration with the Logan Center for the Arts, presents a panel discussion exploring plays from the black theatre canon that are reflective of an African-American blues aesthetic. Discussants are Dr. Ken Warren, University of Chicago and Dr. Mikell Pinkney, University of Florida-Gainesville.

It is moderated by Lincoln T. Beauchamp, Jr., aka 'Chicago Beau,' a Blues artist, record producer, writer and publisher.

FREE and open to the public, it is sponsored by the Center for the Study of Race, Politics & Culture and the Logan Center for the Arts at the University of Chicago and eta Creative Arts Foundation.

The panel discussion is being presented concurrent with eta's season of *Resurrected Works and Reclaimed Music*. The plays to be explored are August Wilson's *Jitney* (which closed October 14th at the Court Theatre) and *Ceremonies In Dark Old Men* (opening November 8th at eta). Says Dr. Pinkney in describing eta's season: "The works of African-American playwrights of the past are resurrected and joined by current writers to illuminate a shared artistic sensibility rooted in the sorrow, pain and joy of blues music and a literary blues aesthetic."

Dr. Mikell Pinkney is an Associate Professor and former Performance Coordinator and Head of Graduate Actor Training in the School of Theatre and Dance at the University of Florida-Gainesville.

Dr. Ken Warren is the Fairfax M. Cone Distinguished Service Professor in the Dept. of English and a faculty affiliate of the Center for the Study of Race, Politics, and Culture at the University of Chicago.

www.etacreativearts.org   773 / 752-3955

14TH INTERNATIONAL JAZZ FESTIVAL

Hesarin teltta 26.–29.4.

"THE SA BOOM BOOM GYPSY TOUR"
Chicago Beau

Chicago Beaun eli siviilinimeltään Lincoln Beauchampin ammatillisten ulottuvuuksien lista kertoo miehestä jo paljon. Hän on milloin huuliharpisti ja laulaja, joskus perkussionisti. Toisaalta hän tunnustautuu myös runoilijaksi, kirjailijaksi, kustantajaksi ja luennoitsijaksi.

Ja kun vielä katsoo syntymäaikaa eli vuotta 1949, voi päätellä jo paljon.

Suuntaan ja toiseen

Onko tässä taas mustaan perinteeseen kiinnittynyt musiikin intellektuelli, joka ei osaa valita todellista ammattiaan. Jonkinlainen Amerikan Tohtori Ammond. Näin saattaisi ajatella ennakkoluuloinen musiikin kuluttaja.

Mutta kun etenee pitemmälle hänen töidensä kirjauksessa, aavistukset kääntyvät jo toiseen suuntaan. Tässä on avoimella asenteella ja ehtymättömällä energialla sonnustettu monilahjakkuus, jonka taidot eivät tunne rajoja.

Jatko antaa tukea jälkimmäiselle tulkinnalle. Meriiteistä löytyy levyjä Sunnyland Slimin, Billy Boy Arnoldin ja Jimmy Dawkinsin kaltaisten blueskuuluisuuksien kanssa. Toisaalla Chicago Beau on löytänyt rinnalleen mustan jazzin suuruksia kuten Archie Shepp ja Art Ensemble Of Chicago. Ei väliä räppääkö hän vai laulaako kotiseutunsa Chicagon mustaa melodiikkaa. Chicago Beaun täytyy olla tärkeä nimi.

- Chicago Beau (voc., harp.)
- Herb Walker (guit., voc.)
- David Michael Clarke (b., voc.)
- Little Henri Lipirinni (guit., voc.)
- Thomas Harris (drs, voc.)

Visio perintöön

Kun lukee vielä listaa keikoista ympäri maailmaa, opetustyöstä maailman yliopistoissa ja kirjoituksista, joita hän on tuottanut ominaan painoksina tai lukemattomissa julkaisuissa, alkaa todella uskoa Chicago Beaun merkittävään rooliin mustan perinnön välittäjänä.

Lopputuloksena kaikista näistä vihjeistä voi päätellä, että Chicago Beau Blues Bandin esitys tarjoaa värikkään ja moniulotteisen vision amerikkaisten mustien musiikkiin ja sanalliseen perintöön. Mikä oli todistettava.

XXIII FESTIVAL INTERNACIONAL de JAZZ

MURCIA • TEATRO ROMEA
1, 2 y 3 de mayo 2003

Jueves 1. 22 h.
- **ROY HARGROVE GROUP (USA)**

- Abdón Alcaraz "Freedom Jazz". Plaza Romea, 13 h.

Viernes 2. 22 h.
- **CHICAGO BEAU and his Wonderful Time Band (USA)**

- Pedro Hita & friends. Plaza Romea, 13 h.

Sábado 3. 21,30 h.
"Mujeres en el jazz"
- **LYNNE ARRIALE TRIO (USA)**
- **ANNIE WHITEHEAD EXPERIENCE (UK)**

- Tempo Libre Quartet. Plaza Romea, 13 h.

ARGENTEUIL EN BLUES

Parc Barron
rue Principale Lachute

VENDREDI / FRIDAY AUGUST 16 AOUT 2019

12 h 00	Parade
13 h 00	Atelier
14 h 00	Jam
15 h 00	Artistes de la relève (sous le chapiteau Subaru)
16 h 00	Pat 'Sonny Boy Gumbo ' Loiselle
17 h 15	Henri Band
18 h 15	Cérémonie d'ouverture
18 h 30	Showcase de Band
20 h 15	Jim Zeller
21 h 45	Woman who Rock & Blues
23 h 00	Jam

PRÉSENTÉ PAR :

Gestion Lakefield inc.
gestionlakefield@hotmail.com

Construction
Rénovation
Excavation
Danny Ouellet Président
450-806-3619
Batitech Une équipe de confiance
R.B.Q 56023229-01

SAMEDI / SATURDAY AUGUST 17 AOUT 2019

10 h 00	Ateliers / Jeux gonflables
13 h 00	Spectacle enfants (Sous le chapiteau Subaru)
14 h 00	Jam
15 h 00	Bands relève
16 h 00	The runaway boy's
17 h 00	Tova
18 h 15	Vocal fest. / Festichant
20 h 00	Rude Mood
21 h 15	J-F FABIANO (INVITÉS JAMES CAMPAGNOLA & CHICAGO BEAU)
23 h 00	Jam

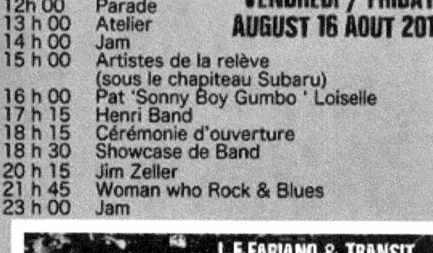
J-F FABIANO & TRANSIT

JAMES CAMPAGNOLA

CHICAGO BEAU

PRÉSENTÉ PAR : MUNICIPALITÉ DE CANTON DE GORE

DIMANCHE / SUNDAY AUGUST 18 AOUT 2019

CÉLÉBRATION GOSPEL (ROBERT LEMIRE) JAMBOREE

www.argenteuilenblues.com
Bienvenue aux V.R. / R.V. Welcome
(Réservation requise / Booking required)

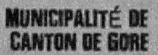

Art Ensemble of Chicago Book, 1999

With Beguine Beauchamp, Dooney Beauchamp, and cousin
Becky Davis next to me
Kansas City, Mo., 2019

My father, Lincoln T. Beauchamp. Sr.
Chicago, Il., circa 1985

My mother, Betty A. Beauchamp
Chicago, Il., circa 1980

With L-R, Linda V. Carter, Aina Louisa Carter, Jessica K. Carter, Toronto, 2019

With Lisa Simone, April Jazz Festival at Espoo, Finland, 2011

With Amina Claudine Meyers, Jazz in Sardegna
Italy, 1992

With Billy Boy Arnold, Chicago, Il., 1993
Photo: James Fraher

With Pharoah Sanders. April Jazz Festival
Espoo, Finland, 2008

With Famoudou Don Moye, left; and Isio Saba
Cagliari, Sardegna, Italy, 1990

With Suski Torvinen, Artists Coordinator
April Jazz Festival, Espoo, Finland, 2007

With SunnyLand Slim, Acme Recording Studio
Chicago, Il., !992.

With Jerry Butler, Chicago, Il., 2011

Guelph Jazz Colloquim Panel
L-R: Roscoe Mitchell, Muhal Richard Abrams, George Lewis,
Moderator, L. Beauchamp
Guelph, Ontario, Canada, 2010

With Ray Frost, Burbank, Calif., 2017

With Elizabeth Nunez, St. Louis, Mo., 1991

With James Campagnola and J-F Fabiano
Ste Saveur, Québec, 2019

With Manuel Franco and Maria Viana
Cascais, Portugal, 2003

With Julio Finn, left; and Russell Prince Arnold
Chicago, Il, 2015

With Raphael left; and Luca O'Neill
Rome, Italy, 2011

With Jason Vivone
Kansas City, Mo., 2015

Blues In Schools Program
Chicago, Il., 1992

My Band, The House Rockers
L-R: David Baily, Franck Rouleau, and
Winston DeLandro
La Boite, Barcelona, Spain, 2002

Back row: L to R: Luigi Amico, Harold Bradley, Luca Casagrande
L to R: Gianni Franchi, Daniele Bombasaro, Marco Corteggiani,
Ranieri di Luca, Famoudou Don Moye
Seated: L to R: Tony Formichella, Isio Saba, Chicago Beau.
Cagliari, Sardegna, 1991

**14 July 2021
Via Zoom
Time For A Change**

It is hard to believe we're having this conversation with Zoom technology. After so many great conversations over the years in different parts of the world, because of this awful disease, Covid 19, we must use every possible means of caution.

I'm thankful for it, believe me. Certainly, if people do the right thing, this Covid can be eradicated. And so, old friend, let us continue where we left off. You were getting restless in San Francisco after such a great period, I'll bet. And I say this because I've known you for years, so I know that you eventually felt that it was time for some type of change.
Yes, You're right. Okay, this is how the next phase begin to take shape. In November of 1974 my mother had breast surgery in Chicago and was recovering well without complications. I asked Rose to come to Chicago with me to meet my family, which she did do. We had a lot of fun in Chicago. We went to clubs, dined well and generally enjoyed the ambiance of the city that continues to change over generations. Back then Chicago was very liveable in terms of the amount of money needed to live well. And the city then, as now, was mostly segregated, not only by race but white ethnic groups as well. The Poles, Swedes, Ukrainians, Irish, Jews, Italians, Indians, Mexicans and others; they all have their districts. Some have signs along the streets identifying the district, like, Ukrainian Village, Little Italy, China Town, Swede Town, Bronzeville, and Little India. And of course, there is no area of the Indigenous people, the Algonquin and Illinois, from whom Chicago

got its name. And there were the housing projects built to isolate Black people and other minorities. These were literally reservations, or urban high-rise prisons. The whole concept was cruel and inhumane. An evil scheme to dehumanize people that was funded by the federal government. The whole point was to make Black people who built the fucking country feel as dejected as possible. But when election time came, the white politicians, mostly democrats, and their Black lackeys would set up polling places in the projects and hand out a few crumbs to get the people to vote for them. Crumbs being anything: a few dollars, a turkey, some reefer, a promise to fix the elevators so you didn't have to walk up twenty flights of stairs. The main projects were *Stateway Gardens, Robert Taylor Homes, Henry Hohner Homes, Cabrini Green, and Ida B. Wells Homes* where I hung out intensely as a child, and some others. Fast forward to the present. Most of those buildings have been torn down, and the real estate values has skyrocketed. The people have been disbursed across the city creating more low-income communities.

Did you show Rose the Black areas?
Absolutely. She saw where I grew up on the westside, where I went to school on the southside, and everything in between. For Rose, experiencing Chicago's urban sprawl with all of its differences was fascinating, and the way Black people were living really angered her. But she could relate because many cities had the same solution for dealing with 'Black Migration.' But we stayed at the Sheraton Chicago on the *Gold Coast,* so we were right in the area with a lot going on and all kinds of people from the neighbourhoods, and tourists would be milling about.

Downtown Chicago is certainly a contrast from where you were living, and it's quite a contrast from the Bay Area. The Chicago vibe is definitely midwestern though, I don't consider it a truly cosmopolitan city because it is so divided ethnically. But it does have a rhythm.
It does, and you're absolutely right. I've encountered people in Chicago who have only been downtown two or three times in twenty years. I've met taxi drivers who go to the airports several times a day who have never been on an airplane. They watch planes come and go, then scratch their heads in awe.

Ha-ha!
Rose was enthralled with the urban sway, the hustle, the rhythm. And so, one evening I brought up the idea of moving to the heart of San Francisco. She was agreeable to the idea but was doubtful that her mother would be. She was right. Not only did her mother object, but I feel totally out of favour, and for a time I was prohibited from visiting her house.

This is like some crazy notions I've heard in Kansas City. People actually refusing to cross a bridge and be north or south of the Missouri River. GeorgiaB was appalled by the suggestion that one of her children would move across the Bay Bridge to San Francisco. The Swisher's spoke about the moving possibility for weeks, until finally one day just after New Year's 1975, GeorgiaB decided to come over to Skyline and confront me personally. She and I had not spoken since Rose brought up the idea when we returned from Chicago. And I think it was only her second visit to our house, we always went to her house for family visits.

You're saying she wanted to confront you face-to-face. She wanted to let you know exactly what was on her mind.
That's right. She let me have it, didn't hold nothing back. She told me I was breaking up her family. She said San Francisco was dangerous, and not safe for Rose's sons. I countered with the fact that Oakland was reputed to be far more dangerous than San Francisco if you chose to believe the press, I also said that San Francisco offered far more diverse schools than Oakland, and that Skyline High School was nearly all white. Well, this went on and for a bit, then she came up with the fact that I had lived in Paris, Greece, and other places probably meant that I was a criminal, and that she was going to call the FBI and have me investigated. I couldn't help but laugh, almost hysterically, but I got a grip on myself. GeorgiaB upset Rose so much that she became even more determined to leave Oakland. I was deep in GeorgiaB's doghouse, and it would be months before we spoke again.

Our lease expired in May, so we had time to look for an apartment. And what we found was an absolutely charming apartment at 1840 Van Ness on the top floor, front. The place had great views, and no structures on either side. It was an older building with an elevator. I recently looked for the building on the internet and found that a huge apartment building had been built where there was once a parking lot. The new structure is blocking all sunlight, and what was once a totally unobstructed view looking all the way down Van Ness towards Lombard. The street directly behind is Polk, which then and now is a Gay and lively street with great restaurants, bars, and nightlife. And the location offered short distances to wherever you wanted to go. The Mission District was 15 minutes away, as was Castro Valley and Noe Valley. Pacific Heights was ten minutes up Van Ness. The Golden Gate Bridge to Marin County was fifteen minutes away. The location was absolutely perfect.

That must have been quite a move from Skyline, you had a house and garage full of things, right?
Actually, Rose and I had sold a lot of things at the San Jose Flea Market, and at our garage sales. So, it wasn't too laborious although we made three trips back and forth across the Bay Bridge. When we finally settled in, it was a great place to call home.

Is it correct to say that your period of repose had officially come to an end?
That's correct. I was totally rejuvenated, and ready to embark upon new beginnings and adventures. Skyline had served its purpose; not only for me, but the rest of the family as well. Moving to San Francisco was exciting for us all, and it didn't take long for us to get into the groove.

What does that mean exactly?
Ha-ha! Well, I knew a few people in town, so we started out by having dinner parties. My friend Milly would come and bring a few new people. Jerome Arnold would come. Marylin Elkins, another friend from Paris, would come by. Then there were the musicians I had been playing with, and the folks from The Great American Music Hall. There was my dear cousin and friend, Jimmie Lee. And so within a couple of months, our crib was happening. I was back! I was going to parties. I attended the Hookers Ball that the wonderful Margot St. James put on. I was playing with Marva Broome and

Maurice at The Reunion on Union Street. I was spending time at *Lawrence Ferlinghetti's City Lights Bookstore.* And it was a fine time for sports in the Bay Area, the Golden State Warriors won the NBA Title in 1975, and the Oakland Raiders were tough contenders in the NFL. There were a lot of different vibes going on that contributed to the areas vibrancy.

I would say that one couldn't ask for a better rebound. How were you able to generate money to afford your lifestyle?
I had a few things going. I had invested a bit of money in Swiss Francs with earnings from the photography business, and I had convinced Rose to do the same. We caught a strong move in the market, quite by chance, and liquidated our positions for a decent profit. I also had music publishing royalties from France. None of this money could be sustaining for a lengthy period of time, but the occasional music gig helped.

I know you have always had an aversion to a regular 9 to 5 job, but in the States you had no celebrity status, no agent to call and get an advance, so you must have had to find some kind of solution when the money was running short.
LaBosse, as you have often heard me say, it is important to trust the *Cosmics*, keep good thoughts, and intentionally harm no one. And so, as fate would have it, one morning I was seated in a café on Polk Street reading the *San Francisco Chronicle.* While perusing the *Want Ads*, just like before when I found the photography business opportunity, a larger than normal ad in bold print got my attention: **WANTED, LONDON COMMODITY BROKERS,** with promises of huge income for those who proved to be qualified, and with sales ability.

Well, the word, London, caught my eye, as well as the earnings potential of more than $50,000 plus annually. I called the offices of Rosenthal & Company, Taylor-Grant Division, located at 1600 South Amphlett, San Mateo. I called and spoke with the office manager, John Dexter, and we agreed to meet the following day.

Goodness, it's hard to imagine you going to a job interview.
I viewed the whole thing as theatre from both sides. I knew that the title, Office Manager, is another way of being an underpaid flunky-in-charge. I really thought this when I contacted someone I knew in the commodity futures business in Chicago that filled me in on Rosenthal, wealthy Texans, Richard Taylor and Cloyd Grant, who were partners in the operation. So when I met Dexter for my interview, I knew he was just an employee possibly with profit sharing, but not a partner in any way.

So, you went in with bit of inside info as to the principles and their latest hustle.
Exactly. I knew about all types of investment strategies and hustles going back to my days in Switzerland when I associated with Bernie Cornfeld's people. And I had traded soybeans as well as currencies myself. But the London thing sounded like it had promise, especially since *London Options* were not regulated at that time.

I met with Dexter, and as I expected, he made exaggerated claims about earning possibilities. That was his job, and he did it well. I then gave him my views on finding good, and lasting salespeople which is that only one in a hundred people interviewed will work out. For every ten people from the hundred interviewed, one may work out somewhat. For every ten some-what's, one may become a true pro, you see what I mean. Hiring and training salespeople is a revolving door that never stops. And dig this, I'm not talking about salaried or paid training, I'm talking commission only. The company paid for offices, WATS lines, a telex machine, a telecopier, a Teletype machine that was a kind of replacement for Ticker-Tape machines, an office manager who received a commission if the office was productive, and a low salaried secretary, that's it. If you complained, bye!

Dexter and I found common ground based on the fact that we were both from Chicago and knew first-hand about the blatant racism that exists there. He told me that to the best of his knowledge, no Black people worked for Rosenthal, who was headquartered in the Chicago Board of Trade building. I had been in that building several times and rarely seen a Black person. Dexter also warned me that the Texans were not used to having any Black people around, in fact, he hadn't seen any.

And so, I started selling London Commodity Futures Options for Robusta Coffee. Call Options only for starters. Some of our readers may remember the big coffee price surge of the mid 70s, this was the basis for millions upon millions of dollars being made.

I knew the deal, so I told Dexter, give me thirty days, and I'll rock the joint, which is exactly what happened. I combined my artistic people skills with Bernie Cornfeld's techniques, along with everything I could learn from him, and boom! After working ten hours a day six days a week, I started to close deals. Some clients called me and closed themselves. I was the first one in the office to make a sale, and that just continued on and on.

How did you find your potential clients?
The system of this type of sales platform is to convince the salespeople that they are part of a rare opportunity to make a lot of money, and to get the ball rolling they should contact all friends and family members to get them to invest before the market takes off and they may miss an opportunity. This of course gets money into the company even if the salesperson fails to sell to anyone else, which was frequently the case. Then there were cold calls from lead providers like Dunn and Bradstreet. I used Dunn and Bradstreet and the telephone directory. I used to randomly call phone numbers in what were considered to be in affluent areas near the office like Hillsboro, Burlingame, and Palo Alto. But the D & B leads could be from anywhere in the United States. My first sale was to a gentleman in Burlingame, and I went to his house to pick up the check. He just wanted to see the person he was dealing with. After a week or so, he increased his investment. I'm happy to say that he made money. And he was a tipper, gave me twenty percent of everything he made.

Was tipping typical?
Perhaps, but I don't think it happened that often, and salespeople never spoke about it, but then again, they weren't closing anyone anyway. I had another client in Fresno that was a big tipper. Both of those guys had really special, exuberant personalities, so their actions made sense.

Anyway, I was doing very well. Well enough for my success to get the intention of the Texas guys, and office manages throughout their thirty plus network of offices across the country. The company was making money, and they were buying so many options they were almost single handidly moving an unregulated market. Word was spreading throughout investors circles, and my job was getting easier. Yet, after about three months, most of the people I started with, my co-workers, had been replaced. I used to listen to them on calls, and I realized that most of them lacked then ability to make the perspective client feel comfortable. That couldn't recognize the openings to make the customer like them and think that they were just another sales grunt trying to make some money. You know, like these asinine robo calls today, a script, that only gets worse if a real person gets on the line.

Please give an example of openings.
Here's an example, the surname of the person you're speaking with. My first sale was a guy whose grandparents had immigrated from Sweden. I told the client the old cliché, America is a nation of immigrants, no matter how much go on about being Americans. So, my client and I talked about Sweden. As it turned out, his grandparents were from Malmo. Boom! We had something to speak about besides the money I convinced him I could make for him. That really worked out because I made him money, he referred other Swedes, and had we many good conversations. One of the major points in selling is learning to listen. But you see the salespeople they just followed a script, almost to the letter, no variations. I would say to perspective customers something like this; 'Jim, thanks for taking my call. I don't wanna be another nuisance reading a script, I want you to listen closely.' 'Huh.' Was a typical response. Then I'd put the phone in waste basket under

my desk and rattle some papers around. 'Jim! Did you hear that?' 'That's the sound of me balling up the company's stupid script! Ninety percent of the time I'd get a laugh and have his attention. Then I may cut into something I knew about where he was: landmarks, sports, food, something. All of this before discussing his investment portfolio.

For me selling options was an easy sell because of my personality, and the investor could never lose more than the price of the option, because that's the nature of investment options. No margin requirements. But in that *bull market,* they could comfortably expect minimally a fifty percent return on their money.

So, money was being made throughout their options selling system, were they having big parties and such?
I heard things, but I certainly wasn't invited to any of their 'Wolf of Wall Street' gatherings. Dexter told me stories that he had heard from other office managers about wild parties in Dallas, and the Colorado office that was located in a resort town, I don't remember which one.

What did Rose think about your success?
She was very pleased about the money, but she never had any interest in how the whole Rosenthal thing worked.

For how did long your success continued?
Things were rolling for quite some time. I started taking a few trips around the country and to Mexico. The long hours I put in at the beginning paid off for months to come.

Does travelling mean that you were starting to feel the need for something new, or to move around again?
Yes, you know me. On a trip to Los Angeles I was driving east on Wilshire Boulevard in Beverly Hills. I was at a stoplight on the corner of Wilshire and Bedford, when I looked up and saw an old friend from Paris crossing in front of me. I couldn't believe my eyes, It was Ray Frost, suited down like he was strolling the Champs Elysees. I shouted, 'Hey Ray, Ray Frost!' he couldn't believe it either. So, I made a quick left onto Bedford, parked, and we caught up.

Ray told me about a few other people that had moved to L A from Paris, including his French girlfriend, Michelle. In fact Los Angeles was full of Paris transplants, some were English, French, American, Italian, Senegalese, and Moroccan. I thought, maybe I should try living in two places, Los Angeles and San Francisco. The two cities have extremely different vibes. Northern and southern California generally have a very different mentality. In fact, at one time the two were legally trying to separate into two separate states.

Did you share your thoughts with Rose?
I did, and she didn't think that was a good idea because she saw that as breaking up our family, whereas I saw it as an expansion. We would have things going on in two cities. I was curious about Los Angeles, Hollywood, and the warm weather lifestyle. Also, Rosenthal had a Beverly Hills office at 8383 Wilshire Blvd.

You have a good and growing circle of friends and acquaintances in San Francisco, and you've now discovered friends in Los Angeles. And some of

your friends know people in both cities from the Paris days, it looks to me like you've got California happening no matter what you decide.

Each city had a different appeal. San Francisco was more cerebral, more oriented towards the arts and social issues, whereas Los Angeles was more pretentious with all of the film industry stuff going on, thousands of 'wannabes' and 'hangers-on' to whatever people they thought could help them gain entrée into Hollywood inner circles. And there was a kind underlying decadence that is part of LA life. My friend, Ray, was deeply immersed in that particular facet, and since he was looking out for my best interest, he encouraged me to spend more time in LA. Also, Earl, the guy that arranged my introduction to Rose was now living in LA. And LA has serious Black neighbourhoods, areas like Crenshaw and Baldwin Hills, and Compton, so that meant lots of good music, like at *Marla's Memory Lane*, and other joints.

Marla's. Who owns that club?

Do you remember a television show in the States called 'The Jeffersons?'

I got it. That's Marla Gibbs' Blues and Jazz club. She acted on the show. Great show. The name sounded familiar, and I heard about the club. I've heard it's one of the hottest spots in Black LA.

Definitely. Her club and others, and the Black community are part of the upside. On the downside, people in LA live in their cars, no real public transportation. Just buses, but an area that big needs a rail system to connect people and create hubs, which they finally have going on now. Like I say about Kansas City, how do you meet when their always in their cars? In LA, it's important to know people when you move there. It is not like Chicago, Paris, Rome or San Francisco where you may have chance encounters or make a new acquittance on a trolley, subway train, or a station café. And as it turned out, I knew more people in LA than I realized at that time.

What did you decide?
Rose and I agreed that I would get a place in LA. This was not a break-up of our relationship, merely an adjustment. Also, with me out of the apartment for a while, Rose's daughter was more likely to visit, which she had been reluctant to do. And I can appreciate her reasoning and feelings on that.

How did you work things out with Rosenthal?
I told John Dexter the office manager what I had in mind. Now, let me say this quickly. I mentioned that Dexter was from Chicago. He was old school Chicago. That means probably most of the white people he knew in Chicago were typical north, northwest side, and Bridgeport racist. Every now and then there would be some kind of friction in Chicago. I'm saying Dexter knew his own people, how they threw around the 'N' word, and much more. And so he warned me about the management in the Beverly Hills office, and some of the other senior members of the company who like to pass through there because it was Beverly Hills. He said that they were 'totally ignorant racist, and motherfucking Dallas hicks.' He said that the office manager, and close associate of the company, John Poole, was the worse. I found that to be true. More on him later.

The Beverly Hills crew knew my reputation, and believe me, some of the white boys had a hard time with that.

When I arrived, John Poole's assistant, a woman by the name of Jingles, assigned me to an office at the end of a hallway. She said that since I was so good, I got a private office. I was fine with that, but I believe it was really for isolation which I welcomed; and that office was pretty small. After about a week, a brought in three new accounts, and rolled over several of my existing ones. The office equity for the week went up. At the morning meeting several brokers praised my efforts. What was supposed to be isolation turned out to be a meeting place where I shared my selling technique with other brokers. You should have seen them gathering at my door, bringing chairs and sitting in the hall because there wasn't much room in the office. This annoyed Poole immensely. The following week I raised even more money; and I had a southern white truck stop owner and his wife visit me from rural Georgia. I had worked my technique on them so well, they didn't realize that I was Black. When I met them in the reception room they were downright floored. The white man shouted, 'You rascal, you!' 'Damn, you good!' 'Yessir, you got me, I never woulda thought you was a Black man.' And so we went to a meeting room, not my small office, and he wrote a check to invest more.

At the next morning meeting, Poole unveiled his racism. He dragged his ugly, lanky, scraggly, cheap suit wearing, uncouth, fifty-something failing ass to the microphone. After a few comments about needing more equity coming in he said, and I quote, 'No matter how big and black you are, you have to remember this office has rules, and I'm here to be sure them rules are respected.' There was a noticeable gasp from some of the forty or so people in attendance. A few of my regulars visitors came to my office and said how out of line they thought that was. I decided to stroll down to the other end of the office and see Poole. His door was slightly open, so I knocked and entered at the same time before he had a chance to say, come in. He said he knew why I was there, but he had to say what he said because some of the brokers were losing sight of why they were there. I said to him: *John you are the manager of one of your company's most successful offices. But today you proved to people at the meeting, no matter how racist some of them may be, that you are weak and petty because you singled out the best, not for doing wrong, because there was no wrong, but because your racist evil ass can't handle a Black person's success and the fact that I'm being admired, and not you. You are in fact, an aberrant low-life, and no matter how loyal a lackey you are, I don't believe your bosses will be pleased when they learn about your behaviour.*

How did you get along with Poole and people at the office after that.
Just basic office cordialness. I did my job. The only person that did better was a wealthy guy, Dee Lee, who had been an insurance broker in Newport Beach. He was bored after leaving that business, but he had hundreds upon hundreds of leads and wealthy family members. In fact, all of his customers were his family members, their friends, and clients of his companies. So, I had told him that he was not a salesperson, but a pampered family brat; and that he should stop boasting. After that he shut the fuck up. And with many co-workers, everything was pretty cool for the most part.

All of this happened shortly after you arrived in LA, how were things outside of the office, where were

you living?

Well, I was living kind of far from anything going on. I wanted to live closer to, or in Beverly Hills, but I didn't have much time look around when I first arrived. A friend knew a realtor out in the San Fernando Valley, and he hooked me up with a four-bedroom home in Canoga Park, in a cul-de-sac on Delco Street. It was quite spacious, and I was able to invite friends and family to stay. In fact, one thing I was finally able to do was to invite my mother from Chicago for a lengthy stay. This was a big thank you to my mom for all she had done for me over the years since my first moment of existence. She really enjoyed herself. She brought a bag of photos from my childhood, and hers that I had never seen before. LaBosse, we had such a great time together. And I took her everywhere: Malibu, Santa Barbara, Universal Studios, Magic Mountain, Santa Monica, LA County Museum of Art, up and down PacificCoast Highway, Mulholland Drive, Topanga Canyon, Laurel Canyon, the *Testimonial Church of God in Christ* in South-Central, and on and on. We dined at the *Brown Derby* in Beverly Hills, where I had a house account and several menu items named after me. That's because I had clients who were related to the restaurant. And I brought my mom to my office, and that really made her proud. Even though she knew I was a nomad at heart and had race issues with management, she could see that I had the ability to navigate and outsmart the system with success.

I remember your parents so vividly. They had come up during a time when you really had to be clever to keep your dreams in sight. And they were up against people more evil than Poole who were in a

position to render great harm.
You're right. And that's what she told me, 'He ain't nothing but a steppingstone, so step on him and keep on pushing.'

Ha-ha! I can hear her saying that. And that's a very mild statement to say about people who think they own you and get extremely irritated when you let them know that they only own themselves, barely.
That's right! And in Poole's case, like many I've known over the years on projects I've been involved with, when their white male narcissistic neuroticism takes a beating, they crack. But what is hilarious to me in when you have several of them in a room in a decision-making discussion. They be sooo, damn fragile, and they be trying to make each other angry.

How long did this business hold your interest?
Actually, this business itself, as a vehicle to make money, only held my interest for a short time. When I examined all of the techniques used to predict markets, like fundamental and technical analysis, I realized that much of it was no more than a *Daily Racing Forum* for investors. You can study shit day and night and still lose. You can take a shot in the dark and win. True factors, like poor harvest or weather patterns have some validity. Other markets move because everybody expects it, plays it, and of course you get a move. Some players have inside info. I think coffee was a good bet because of the circumstances under which coffee is produced, which is why I stopped trading it.

We've spoken a length about this, please share your thoughts.
I was speaking with a friend in Paris, Mahmood, who

was from Cote d'Ivoire, and often contributed to a publication called *Présence Africaine.* We were talking about how the French would exploit Africans for cheap labour, and often put them up in dormitories. I told him my story about the time I gave cigarettes and cash to African workers I saw in blue uniforms working in a hole in ground in the wealthy 16th Arrondissement in Paris. The white French overseer ordered me away and tried to stop me from talking with my African brothers. I made it clear to him in English and French that I wasn't taking orders from his ass. Mahmood said that what I witnessed in Paris was the adult version of cheap child labour that takes place in many African, and other countries. Then we spoke about coffee. From Mahmood I learned more about the viciousness of the European footprint in Africa. I was already well studied in many aspects, but when Mahmood so vividly described children working ten-hour days for a dollar or less a day, and how entire families became indentured servants, slaves basically, to French, Belgian, Portuguese, German and other plantation owners in order to supply the American, German, and French coffee appetites. I learned everything that the Rosenthal people had passed over.

Was there ever any discussion at Rosenthal about how coffee was brought to market?
We got alleged crop reports that spoke about weather conditions, and an occasional news update that may have mentioned a deal struck with an American importer and some plantation. But there was never any discussion about how labour-intensive growing coffee is.

And so, a few days after speaking with Mahmood, at

the morning meeting I brought up child labour in Africa, and elsewhere. I prepared a 500-word essay that addressed child labour and exploitation. I copied it and passed it around at the meeting. I asked management, which on this particular day consisted of a few higher-ups in from Dallas, why they never mentioned the suffering behind their newly found wealth in the coffee markets; and by that time the company had expanded to cocoa also, which followed coffee a bit in the speculative markets.

None of them good southern Christians had any sympathy. Some used the defence that trading is just something on paper, and speculators rarely, if ever take delivery. I argued back that a basic premise of the market is hedging, which is a tool used by people directly involved in a particular market, such as growers and wholesalers. And if the growers were hedging against losses, then why are illegal and cruel child labour not a part of the profit chain. Not a word from them motherfuckers. The meeting moved on to other business.

Was there any discussion later amongst the brokers?
Oh quite a bit. And some of the ladies in the office appeared to be quite concerned. Some said that they had no idea, but once they thought about it, they could see it happening. So, people gathered around my office, and others and myself talked about it lunch a couple of times. But anyway, I decided to develop an exit strategy from Rosenthal. I was scheduled to take the required Broker's Exam for the major exchanges, so I took it, and passed. I wanted to get that done just in case I wanted to participate in other aspects of the business. Then I advised my clients who were *in the money* to liquidate.

With some I could share my reasons, and with others, no. There was no money in the trades as my commission was earned when the client purchased the option. Of course, I made money when I rolled their profits into more options. Another thing happened in those final days, John Poole was replaced by a much more pleasant fellow, C.W. Timmons. The entire office breathed a sigh of relief when it was announced the Poole's wretched ass would not be returning. Within a week of Poole's leaving I announced my resignation. Timmons, who wanted to keep the offices numbers up, implored me to stay on. I explained my reasons, to which seemed indifferent; and I was also tired of talking on the phone. I was detached from the people who worked there. I had accomplished my mission of learning more about the workings of some aspects of the financial system. I become a Commodity Futures Trading Commission licensed broker by passing the test that most failed. And indirectly, I learned from Les Rosenthal that taking on the Government is something not to fear when you know your being challenged because of politics, overpaid regulators trying to appear busy, and nothing more.

You were done!
This was 1977. A few years later I traded Interest Rate Futures and Gold for a few months with a firm in Chicago. Theoretically, the gold was already mined and stored in various banks, vaults, and Treasury departments of various countries represented on the exchanges. But the child labour and trafficking problem still exists within high profit 'greed' industries: precious metals and stones, oil, coffee, sugar, etc. It's hard to get around it, the best thing one can do is to try and deal with businesses that claim to practice fair trade, and source responsibly. I can't vouch for any of them, but

there is an organization, The Borgen Project, which may have useful information regarding child labour. Anyway, that was it for me. My explorations were over, and I learned a lot. It was back to what I love; music, writing and other arts.

What was your next move?
When my lease on the house in Canoga Park expired I moved to West Hollywood, and that was quite by luck. One day I was driving down Fountain, and I decided to make a right on Sweetzer for no reason other than to look around. As soon as I turned the corner, I saw a man putting a For Rent sign in the yard of 1286 N. Sweetzer. I got out of my car, spoke with him, went upstairs and took a look at the apartment, and came back downstairs. We drove to his office in his Persian Carpet Store on La Cienega, signed the lease, and that was that. Unbelievable. Top floor with two bedrooms, two baths, living and dining rooms, great kitchen, balconies, for $550.00 a month.

That's a great location. Just a few blocks south of Sunset, close to Beverly Hills, and Century City. And you could shoot down La Cienega all the way to the airport of you wanted. How did the move go?
A couple of more people had turned up in LA from the Paris days, among them was David 'Doc' Robinson, who is the singer on the hit song, 'Dancing in the Moonlight,' by King Harvest. David had a large van, so I got him and one of his buddies to help me move. We had a moving party, lots of fun, and good memories to share. And so I started a new phase that would lead to unexpected changes in my life.

What happened in West Hollywood that brought

about changes?
Well, since leaving Rosenthal I time on my hands. I had time to reevaluate my direction. Initially, I was thinking about living another year in California, then returning to Paris or maybe Rome, and eventually spending some time travelling in Africa. I did do that, but some years later.

My friend, Ray, had broken up with his lady friend, Michelle, from Paris, so I rented him a room in my apartment. Together we got into the Southern California lifestyle. A typical day was a few sets of tennis in the mid-afternoon or go to the beach at Santa Monica or Malibu with lady friends. Then have ladies over for dinner, as Ray and I both have excellent culinary talents. The nights were long and full of pleasant activities. Often there were parties going on in the Hollywood Hills, Beverly Hills, or maybe right in the neighbourhood. Unlike now, the neighbourhood wasn't as developed. Melrose Avenue was commercial, but not overly so. Santa Monica Boulevard had activity but was also not overly commercialized. There were clubs like the *Troubadour* where you could run into most any celebrity. I ran into *Fred Astaire* and *Ron Wood* the same evening. The Jazz Bar in the *Hyatt Hotel on Sunset* was always popping. Then there are the Beach towns. The *Laguna Beach Hotel* had a Jazz Brunch on Sunday afternoons that was really popular. The sun and ocean, good music and food. Comfortable seating, a great way to spend time on a Sunday. And there was *Howard Rumsy's Concerts by the Sea Jazz Club.* The seating was a little tight, but it was a great venue right by the ocean in Redondo Beach. I caught Pharoah Sanders there, tremendous. We had friends with beach-front houses in Manhattan Beach and Hermosa Beach. Ray begin a relationship with a great lady, *Lisa Hyman*, whose late husband, *Walter A Hyman,* along with *Alan King,* were producers of *Barbra Streisand's* tours and concerts in the 1960s. The dinner parties at Lisa's were always lively with stimulating conversation across cultures and experiences.

Another friend Johnnie J, showed up from Atlanta via Chicago, and became the manager of a small, but extremely vibrant apartment complex directly across the street from my place called the *Fountain Lanai*. That place was full of aspiring actors, models, athletes, and others looking for that big break! It was also a place for those with habitual 'extra' roles who were frustrated because a bigger role with significant money had never happened, in some cases for decades. This was often the poolside chatter, It's kind of sad in a way to think of a Hollywood career being mostly casted in mob scenes, or one of hundreds of people running away from a volcano eruption.

I recall speaking with you about meeting ladies who told you they were to be married in a few days and wanted to have a final fling. You also told me about attending weddings where the groom and his buddies got so drunk that the ignored wife had no choice but to resume her previous activities whilst wearing the pure white wedding gown that no than more a couple of hours earlier, she had sworn fidelity to her now drunk and boisterous husband.
Ha-ha! Let me assure you that lifting a brides dress in some hidden chamber of a wedding reception hall, with a clear view of the drunken groom carrying on merrily with is comrades a stone's throw away, is an unparalleled high that will never be forgotten. LA decadence is

well known in movies, the gossip rags, and books. Most of it, even if fictionalized, is close enough to what's real. I managed to immerse myself until total exhaustion, then finally, boredom set in.

The alure of Southern California is certainly tempting, and it's perfectly understandable why people remain there even with the high cost of living. I'm one of the few who after a time, was tired of LA, because in my opinion, there's no depth. There's a lot of superficiality with wanna be stars, models, and so on. But for me, there was nothing I could really hold on to. And like I said, I think if you are born there, grow up there, and have friends and family, it's probably different. I think ninety-nine percent of the people I knew were from somewhere else. In fact, I met more LA natives somewhere other than in LA. I knew a couple of families that were Orange County natives, and I married a lady who was not from LA, but had lived there since before High School, and married a Los Angelino. That lady is the mother of my son, Kevin, her name was Rose Ingraham, she passed away in 1993 in Los Angeles.

Yes, I recall. I believe you were in San Remo, Italy at the time.
That's correct, and my son, Kevin, was in Roma on his way to meet me and the Art Ensemble of Chicago at our concert in San Remo when he got the news. He headed back to LA to be with family members. A sad occasion. Our family had lots of good times.

You married Rose Ingraham, what happened with your relationship with Rose Swisher?
Rose Swisher and I remained great friends, but there were changes taking place all around her. Her eldest

son, Bill moved to Seattle. Jacob, who lived with me for a while in West Hollywood while he was attending *Art-Center College of Design* in Pasadena, eventually he moved to Paris where he received valuable tutelage from my old friend, Julio Finn. And her daughter was also back and forth between Seattle and San Francisco. As you can see, her children were choosing their own paths, and the apartment in San Francisco was not appealing to her anymore. Then Rose experienced a profound epiphany. She decided that she wanted to live closer to nature. She moved to a small town on the *Russian River* and begin studying to become a Buddhist Monk. We remained friends until she passed away in 2015 in Seattle. In 1978 our San Francisco scene came to a close.

How did you meet Rose?
A singer I knew, Leona, introduced me to Rose. That was in November 1977. I remember being in the kitchen cooking when I heard them all coming up the steps. It was Leona with her two kids, and Rose with hers, Kevin and Kecia. Beautiful children, just running around and playing. Interacting with the adults, laughing and jumping around. They were the way children should be, happy and enjoying being children. Anyway, Rose and I got along well immediately. After hanging out together around six months, we decided to move in together, to be family. We rented a house on Perkins Lane in Redondo Beach.

I'm guessing that by now, you must have exhausted saved money from your brokerage days, is that right? Now you have another family, how did you manage?
Well, I had a couple of decent hustles. One was working

as a Car Sales Location Manager for an international car rental company. I had this gig in Long Beach, then was transferred to Ontario Airport. And the other was refurbishing certain classic automobiles for a decent profit. The company sold its rental cars, some with very low milage; and all of the cars came with a service history. There was no haggling over prices as they were fixed by model and year. If I sold a car to a customer who happened to be driving a car I thought I could fix up and sell, I made an offer outside of office hours. I remember a customer had a beautiful 1966 Thunderbird. I bought it for $500.00. Another had a Dodge convertible, I bought it for $600, and so that was a good side hustle. And these deals were only done after the company business was over if any had occurred. In fact, the deals took place at my house or my customers. And so a buddy, Sergio, and I would take cars down to Tijuana, Mexico and have them painted, completely detailed, and whatever was needed. I sold the Thunderbird for $3000, and the others at a good profit. Another benefit was that as Sales Location Manager, I got to drive any car I wanted except cars classified as luxury vehicles like Lincoln and Cadillac. And I got free gasoline wherever there was a corporate location. Great perks!

Rose had not seen her father in years, and Kevin had never met his grandfather. I had some time off and was able to drive a very nice Buick across the country to New Jersey, so Kevin and Rose could meet family. Also along the way, we stopped in Chicago, and Rose got to meet my family. It was really a beneficial trip, not only because of family, but adventure on the road: the restaurants, New York City, Kevin and his mom seeing the Atlantic Ocean for the first time, going up high-rise buildings like Sears Tower in Chicago, and the Empire

State Building in New York. These kinds of buildings didn't exist in LA at the time. You, know, earthquakes! A lot of fun miles, regrettably, Kecia didn't want to come along, she preferred to stay in LA with her biological father which is understandable.

It seems that your wild days are becoming more and more intermittent. You are becoming more and more a family man, a husband and father. With Rose Swisher, you were also in a similar role. When you think back, what comes to mind about your behaviour and life philosophy that guides you?
I think many, including me, like to extend our own family experiences from are youth, but not always positive. I may not have agreed with some things about my childhood, but the overall take away is quite positive. I had inspirational parents, who loved my sister and my childhood innocence. And that fact alone was something that I wanted to share, and even expand upon in my families, as I had relationships with women who already had children.

As we all know, many households are in a state of turmoil. The children are abused, the parents are negative alcoholics or dope heads. The children's innocence gets swallowed up by their environment created by fucked-up parents, who are in many cases living out an extension of their own damaged childhood. It's like an unbroken chain of neuroses that passes from generation to generation.

My life philosophy, as you asked, is to take family life seriously, and not persecute the innocent. Now, that can be a challenge because it takes both parents to be like minded in this endeavour, and that can be difficult if one of the parents is hiding a miserable past the only reveals itself over time to the detriment of the innocent. One never knows how things will turn out, but when the children grow up and look back, I want them to have positive recollections about my participation.

My life philosophy is not fixed. I grow and learn from many including children, wives, friends, elders, ancestors, the Cosmics, and the day-to-day life experiences.

Certainly, no relationship is perfect. So many struggles, and the unexpected can occur. We've all had to make difficult decisions, life altering decisions. I've always appreciated your philosophy of 'staying in the mix' if possible, and if not, try to readdress issues if and when everyone wants to talk it through.
Yes, and hopefully all involved can find a balance, and be healthy and happy.

Well continuing, how did things go in your domestic life?
Rose and Kevin liked Chicago. On the drive back to LA we talked about the possibility of leaving California for Chicago. And on New Year's Eve 1979, we arrived in Chicago. We started 1980 off in Chicago. We lived in the *Blackstone Hotel* on Michigan Avenue, the same hotel where the outstanding venue, the *Jazz Showcase* was located. At the time the hotel was steeped in luxury, and furnishings from the bygone eras of design. I noticed Art Deco influenced furnishings, and the architecture of the building has been described as neoclassical Beaux-art. Over the years the hotel had been regularly frequented by the celebrities of all sort including entertainers, politicians, and gangsters. John Kennedy, Al Capone, Louis Armstrong, Lena Horne, and Booker T.

Washington, who was the hotels first Black guest. Actually, for anyone who is interested Chicago history, there are many stories connected to the *Blackstone* if one wants to probe around a bit.

I can't leave this out. Our stay at the *Blackstone* was a gift from my father, who figured that we should have a bit of comfort before diving into whatever it was going take to make Chicago home.

How long were living there?
We were there nearly a month, then we found a lovely apartment on the Northside of Chicago, at Clarendon and Bittersweet Place, one block from Marine Drive, and the lakefront. There, family life just grew. Kecia came to live with us and the next thing you know, the kids are not kids, they are teenagers bordering on being young adults. As a family we certainly had some good times, even with the fun people who lived in the building. I worked quite a bit for my Dad, and Rose got a job at a gourmet wine and cheese store, which sold all types of interesting food and drink. Kevin went to a Fine Arts Academy in the Old Town area and was star on the Chicago Park District Wresting Team.

I also continued selling cars that I would by at auction, or have a friend in LA ship me clean, no rust cars to sell in Chicago, were the weather and salted streets in the winter could take a toll on a car's appearance. Here's an interesting story. My partner in LA sent me a right-hand drive *1969 Mercedes SE*. Not many people in Chicago had seen this car, especially with the English design. The car got a lot of interest, but the gentleman who finally bought it became a victim of a heinous murder. His name was *Werner Hartmann,* and he was a very good person, who, unfortunately got tangled up with the wrong woman who plotted his brutal demise for shear greed. Werner had become a successful car stereo dealer. He started out selling car stereo equipment and music tapes at flea markets, and eventually made millions with his installation shop. This is what he related to me. But the whole story is complicated and has been told by many. One thing I recall is that one day I was heading to the Chicago and Northwestern Station in Chicago, and I saw a headline in a newspaper vending machine which read, Northbrook Millionaire Killed, and I just had the feeling that it was Werner. I can't relate the entire story here but Googling the Werner Hartmann murder renders a great deal of results.

Tragic, and Evil, the Hartmann story.
Indeed. Continuing. Occasionally, I would sit-in at a Chicago Blues club and bring the family when allowed. Some clubs would let children in if accompanied by a parent. It was also during this period that my great friend and inspiration, harmonica player, Big Walter Horton passed away. He and Rose were quite fond if each other. After Walter's funeral, Rose and I went to *Killers Keyhole Lounge*, in the *Ritz Hotel*, on the southeast corner of Oakwood Boulevard and King Drive. We had several drinks and toasts to Walter's life and Ancestor Brilliance. This was December 15, 1981.

Unfortunately, some circumstances came into play that caused Rose and I to grow apart. I won't go into all that happened, but I'll will say that complications from outside elements that could not be resolved were at the core of the breakup. And the whole thing was heartbreaking for all of us

I remember you were pretty saddened and exhausted by the whole affair. What was your next move?
For about a year before we broke up I had been working in a travel agency on the side that required selling skills, and I was also selling investments, and working in an art gallery on Michigan Avenue, near Ohio Street, right on the Gold Coast. I learned quite a bit about the art business, and used my sales techniques I learned in the options business, with a twist. I wasn't selling over the phone disguising my voice and other closing techniques; now, I stood alongside the customer speaking about an art piece. Me, a six foot-four-inch Black man selling only white customers a piece of art.

Ha-ha! How did you manage?
I found common ground like I did on the phone, and that put the customer at ease. I did the same with an art buyer, and I could put the customers inside of the piece of art by listening to them.

Which means you were able to help the customer weave their own imagination around and in the piece until they really wanted to buy it.
That's right! I sold pieces by Chagall, Dali, Alvar, Rothe, and many others. And I had learned something new, the art business.

When Rose and I split I went back Los Angeles. I got a vendor's license and opened a stall on *Venice Beach.* I had become a registered are dealer before I left Chicago. I sold mostly framed art and music posters at my stall, and more valuable works by appointment. This was a good way to ease the sadness of the breakup, as Venice beach has unlimited visuals, as well as sun, sea, beautiful people, the pleasing scent of pleasure, and the rhythm of beach life. Nice! Really Nice!

Where were you living during this period?
I had no fixed address for a minute. I was crashing at Jim Conley's house for a while. Jim is the great saxophone player who wrote *Nite-Lite* and worked for a long time with *Memphis Slim.* His house in Hawthorne was a fun and stimulating place to be. He certainly had interesting guests, from musicians to strippers who worked in a nearby club, that Jim called the *Naked House.*

I met Jim in Paris in 1970, and we are on a couple of albums together with Julio Finn, and a CD I produced called *Chicago Blues Night* with various Chicago Blues musicians back in 1991. When I wasn't at Jim's I was out in Calabasas with another friend, Jennifer S., a great lady that I met years earlier when I was at Rosenthal.

This was kind of recovery period, shake the Blues period for you. How long did this period last?
Well, I decided to use this period to make some serious changes in my life, physically, and spiritually in terms of discipline. In summer of 1984, the Olympics were in LA. There were events taking place at different venues around LA, and the main venue was the LA Coliseum for Track and Field events, as well as opening and closing ceremonies. I was inspired. I decided to quit smoking cigarettes. I smoked my last cigarette on July 4, 1984, a couple of weeks before the Games started. Then I signed up for aerobics classes at Richard Simmons Anatomy Asylum. I played lots of tennis, and cut-

out hard booze. I was thirty-five years old and didn't want to get any older without trying to get into top shape.

Was your beach business still thriving?
I kept it going until the Olympics were over. After the tourist left town, I decided to focus on my return to music, staying in shape, and resuming travel. In fall of 1984 I went to Montego Bay, Jamaica for a month to visit my daughter, Jessica, and her mother, Linda, who was now married to a fine gentleman, Glenn Nelson.

And how was that trip?
It was fine, a precursor to the making of amends with Linda which would gradually follow. It was great to spend time with Jessica, because up to that point, it had been difficult for Linda and me to resolve our differences. But we did and have been great friends for years.

After Jamaica, I travelled to Ensenada in Baja, California for about a month, just relaxing, swimming, playing tennis and writing. On the way back to LA I stopped in San Diego and sat in with local musicians, and Chicago Blues artist, Cash McCall at Jim Croce's nightclub. Nice club, nice town.

All of this time on the southern California coast, I'm imagining myself living in Dakar, Rome, Paris or maybe summers in Montréal and winters in Senegal, but only after I establish myself in Chicago. My point being that when many of the cats my age were starting out, they were in Chicago. I was not, I was everywhere else, mostly Paris. I'm thinking that it's important for me to establish myself with the Chicago Blues elders, some of whom I knew already like Sunnyland Slim, Jimmy Dawkins, Johnny Shines, Koko Taylor, Pinetop Perkins, Lafayette Leak, and others. But I needed to make an indelible mark on the Chicago scene by making meaningful contributions to Black culture, especially in the realm of Blues. Once again, it was time to say goodbye to LA. One day I loaded up my Mustang II and headed east to Chicago.

How long did it take you to settle in?
I arrived in Chicago in September of 1985. I moved into Marina Towers on a sublet basis for a couple of months, then I shared a house with a friend in Oak Park.

I decided to visit Kenya, and Senegal, the east and west of Africa. I flew on Pan Am that used to have a flight from JFK to Dakar, Monrovia, Lagos, and Nairobi. In Kenya because of time restraints, I couldn't see as much of this beautiful country that I wanted to. I would have had to stay at least two years. I was bothered by the fact that I was an unwilling tourist. I had never been a tourist before. And so to minimize that effect, I quickly learned as much about the lay of the land as I could and demonstrated some familiarity when asked a question by actual tourist. Ha-ha! Anyway, I rented a Suzuki car that was sort of styled like a Jeep. I have a hard time fitting in the driver's seat of Jeeps, but the Suzuki front seat was impossible. So, the car rental mechanic removed the driver's seat, and I drove using the back seat.

I'm sure you got a few looks!
I headed for the *Masai Mara* without hotel reservations, but the Suzuki was equipped with a rooftop tent which I used a few times. And when I did, curious wildlife vis-

itors looked on to see who was on their turf. At night, there were sounds from animals that I was told were hyenas. Several officials advised me against sleeping atop the Suzuki. I finally checked into a lodge, and believe me, it was the most white place I've ever been. This lodge was a white man's colonial retreat. The whole white safari mindset of hunting, even though not allowed, ordering Black servants around, calling grown men 'boy,' and at night after a few drinks, dancing around mocking Kenyan dancers. And the Kenyans were putting up with that shit. I guess they were getting paid, hopefully. I mean the price for a night in some of those places can be well into the thousands. I just hope the owners are African.

Finally, what was happening sank in. This is tourism in Kenya. Providing a wildlife African fantasy for white people, Black servants included. And as I later learned, many locals were getting paid, but not nearly enough for the bullshit they have to tolerate. But the Kenyans have been dealing with the British arrogance for a long time and know how to deal with them. The Mau-Mau uprising, and culture is very much alive in the minds of many Kenyans. This was my takeaway from speaking with the Black manager at the *Boulevard Hotel* in Nairobi, who I watched endure a barrage of racist insults from a British tourist. He let me know that he wasn't going to let that ranting, ignorant fool get him arrested. Makes sense, since there are so many like that guy, and that situation could happen at any time.

Unfortunately, as I said earlier, I didn't have a lot of time, or money for that matter, to explore the country, or interact with the people as much as would have liked. But still, there were some interesting occurrences. A vendor at the Equator line was selling record albums. He told me that I was the first Black American he had ever met. He had some questions about the music he was selling. He wanted to know if *Stevie Wonder, The Temptations, Gladys Knight,* and *Michael Jackson* were Black, because there were no pictures on the albums he was selling. They were much like those recordings in the US that had white people dancing at a beach party. I confirmed their Blackness, and the man went wild! 'I knew it!' He shouted. 'These white people that give these to us sell don't say anything about them being Black!' He exclaimed. And I told him that once upon a time in the United States, the exact same thing happened, white people trying to downplay who we are by trying to remove the possibility of a Black being appreciated for anything. I told him about *Race Records* in the USA at one time. I mean this brother was grateful for the info. I didn't by any records, I gave him some cash for himself. And you see, there are places in the world so remote that people don't have a clue about things we take for granted.

Another thing was a misconception about money among some people. I was having coffee at a café on Kenyatta Street where I met some really nice young men. We were having an interesting chat about their country when one of them told me that they needed to get to Zimbabwe for work and wanted to know if I could help them out. I asked what they needed. They said around ten-thousand dollars each would be perfect. They looked at me in total disbelief when I said that I didn't have that much money anywhere. And one of them said that's not much, you don't have that on you? I explained how long it would take the average worker in the US to make $10,000, let alone save that much, and then be able to give it away. I came up with ten years, maybe. They honestly had no concept, and I think it was because of the large numbers in their currency that was pretty much worthless outside of Kenya. 10,000 shillings today is about $90.00. I wish I had been able to do something. These gentlemen were from *Kibera*, an area of unbelievable poverty that was created by the British solely for the purpose of denigration, repression, and a resource for cheap labour. Many people in *Kibera* live on less than a dollar a day.

Yes, the European colonizers way of creating poverty wherever they went while enriching themselves. We know the story, from Nairobi, to Brazil. Across indigenous lands and cultures, exploitation is the goal. The contrasts in Africa are amazing, from Safari resorts, gold and diamond mines and many types of mineral wealth, to the Kiberas, in nearly every African country.

I went to Kibera, I've been in favelas in Brazil, and I've never seen such poverty in Europe. But I have seen Catholic churches and royal palaces adorned with stolen wealth. And I've visited museums that exhibit, warehouse, and buy and sell centuries of creations by indigenous people from around the world.

Hopefully, in time, indigenous peoples' creations will be returned to them. And Africa can enjoy its own wealth that has feed Europe's greed for centuries. For how long where you in Kenya?

A total of ten days. I spent the last evening at one of the bars at the *New Stanley Hotel*. I had read a bit about the hotel's history, it has been a part-time residence to some extremely prominent people including Earnest Hemingway and others of that same arrogant ilk that loved to come to Africa and compensate for their impotency by imposing their Euro-arrogance, which is actually an inferiority syndrome, by killing animals for kicks, and enjoying being waited upon by occupied people. I really wanted to see the Stanley's opulence and observe the patrons. This hotel for many years was meeting place for politicians, royalty, clergy and others who shaped colonialism in Kenya.

I also met an Indian couple who were visiting family in Nairobi. They gave me a brief history of Indians migrating to Kenya during the colonial era when Great Britain also occupied India. The British used Indians primarily from *Gujarat,* for cheap labour since the 17th Century. That's over 300 years that Kenya has been a part of the *Indian Diaspora,* and around thirty percent of Nairobi's population is Indian, which is quite noticeable when walking around the city. Overall, the Indian community seems to be prosperous. It was good to get this info first-hand from people who have had family living in Kenya for several generations. That's it for me in Nairobi, at The New Stanley Hotel, just a few kilometres from Kibera.

I flew to Dakar, a fine city with an urban rhythm as well as an incredible feeling of familiarity as I walked down the streets or sat in Cafes. I saw people that could be my twin brother or sister. I saw my father's and my mother's face and body types in so many people. I knew I was in the place of my Ancestors. The reason for my trip was to go to the *Grande Marché* and buy a balafon, boubous and anything else I could get on the plane, and to visit *Gorée Island,* where our captured Ancestors were kept in pens before being loaded into the bowels of slave ships, chained, shackled, and brought to the Americas.

I know that feeling you get in Gorée, and those slave castles in Ghana, and other places along the coast of West Africa, that leaves me feeling like my insides have been ripped out. I can feel the Ancestors swirling and the Cosmics providing strength to survive in a new land without hope of ever seeing home or family again.
I did what I sat out to do. And for a little irony, near the boat landing to head to Gorée, who do I see? George Schulz, the Secretary of State for the US, and his entourage. I thought, I guess he wanted to have a first-hand look at where the Black slave people power originated to create America's wealth, and report back to his boss, Hollywood cowboy, socialite, homophobe, and racist, president Ronald Reagan.

Well said, Beau. A kind of model for Donald Trump. I really wish I had been able to spend more time in Dakar, and some of the outlying areas. Here's something that happened though just outside Dakar. Along with friends who I knew in Dakar, Virgil W., and Mahadi W., I went to a small café near a brook, like a small river. There was a guy panning for gold in the river. After about five minutes of panning, he had enough gold for a meal. He had the gold fragments in a cloth, gave them to the café manager I suppose, and ordered a meal. My friend Mahadi said that was quite common. And he added, just imagine how much gold there was when the French first colonized Senegal.

Oh yes, minerals and precious metals, precious stones and more, rich Africa! Europeans were kill-

ing each other almost more than they were killing Africans in order to get their greedy mitts on the wealth first!

And in the Americas, they went totally gold crazy!

**29 July 2021
Via Zoom
Excerpts From Book 1, Too Much UnConvenience, and Onward**

LaBosse, hopefully this is our last techno-meet! With vaccines and boosters, and wearing mask, and the populous growing wiser, maybe we can soon meet in person again, maybe Roma.

Maybe, although travelling isn't as easy for me as it once was. Beau, you may have to come to Tahiti. Anyway, let's roll. You're back from your trip to Kenya and Senegal. Next move?
Once back in Oak Park, I begin putting my plans into place. Musically, I started playing a few gigs with *Clarence Wheeler and the Enforcers.* I started the *Chicago Beau Blues Band,* and we started doing a few gigs locally, but I avoided the usual Blues clubs because I couldn't see myself asking a club owner if I could work for next to nothing. I did place some venues that I liked including *Close Encounters* on Rush street that paid what I asked, and it wasn't considered a Blues bar. I also played the *Cotton Club* on south Michigan Avenue, a Black owned club that catered to a mostly Black clientele. I did gigs at the Chicago Cultural Centre, and a few colleges in Illinois and Wisconsin. The Oak Park newspaper, *Oak Leaves,* featured me on the cover of an issue, and a full story on my views regarding the business of Blues. Also during this period I had a column in a multi arts newspaper, *The Chicago Musicale,* which featured writing, photography, reviews and more from Chicago contributors. That newspaper struggled at times, and I hated to see it fold. I think the publisher, *Don Kaufman,* and editor, *Andy Van Roon,* really did an

an excellent job. As a result of working at *The Musicale,* I met many good people, learned a lot about the publishing business, and sold advertising also, which served as my introduction to Chicago businesses. After The Musicale folded, many of my advertising clients stayed with me when I started *Literati Chicago,* and *The Original Chicago Blues Annual.*

Beau, we spoke about connecting sections from Book 1. I think this is a good place to do it because our readers can get read about a major part of your publishing history,

Readers, what follows is a revised excerpt from *Too Much UnConvenience,* pages 178 to 188. Afterwards, LaBosse and I will resume our current conversation.

**Hilton Nordica,
Reykjavik Blues Festival, Reykjavik, Iceland
19-21 March 2016**

Was it surprising that you received good support for your new venture?

No, it wasn't. The process of looking for support was defining. I approached people who made it clear that they wanted nothing to do with anything Black, not even if they stood to profit. But I'm grateful to *The Art Ensemble of Chicago* and *Famoudou Don Moye* for their funding help; and also, *Bill Gilmore, Rob Hecko,* and *Pete Crawford,* owners of *B.L.U.E.S., Blues Etc.,* and all who, from the beginning, always had an advertising presence in my publications. Some people and organizations were overwhelming in their support. To name a few: the *DuSable Museum, Paul Freeman and his Chicago Sinfonietta, Rizzoli Books, Guild Books,*

Nicole Smith, the State of Illinois, the City of *Chicago, WFMT Radio,* and *Floyd Webb's Backlight Film Festival.* Support came in many forms, from contributing writers to staff members. And some local journalists heaped praise on the project, among them David Witter, and David Whiteis. Many good people helped my vision of publishing a literary magazine become reality.

Did you gather momentum as a publisher after the first issue of Literati?
Interesting question, because it has one of those yes and no answers. There was lots of interest from the literary community, we created a buzz. Submissions rolled into the mailbox daily. But the old problem was always present, money. We received grants and sold advertising. And my wife, *A.C.,* and I had a daughter, *Honorée Dakar,* born on January 17, 1988, the same month Literati made its debut at Rizzoli and was circulated by Ingram Periodicals. But expenses far outweighed revenue. And we were criticized by certain snooty ass, backwards thinking, not-for-profit minded people for selling advertising. Another thing was the technology was nowhere near what it is today for printing. In fact, *Literati Number 1* was traditionally typeset, and with colour separations. For *A.C.* and me this was all totally new. But it didn't take long to figure things out, to get on board with the latest technology available at that time. And you know, learning has its cost, and mistakes can be costly. We paid a lot of money for *Literati Number 1*, much more than necessary. Issue number 2 cost quite a bit less, but I soon realized why universities, who have a constant source of funding, are the main publishers of literary magazines. So, after Number 2, I tried a different approach. I decided to create a glossy, large format magazine with certain writings

translated into Italian, and later French and Spanish. I called the new magazine *Literati Internazionale*; and I did it in collaboration with *Southern Illinois University at Edwardsville*. That was thanks to the efforts of *Eugene B. Redmond,* who was Poetry Editor, and Associate Publisher. SIUE paid a great deal of the expense, but they wanted to know what was done with the advertising money. They couldn't grasp that the magazine was a source of income for my family. I mean other than my love for what I was doing, I had a family to feed. They just couldn't comprehend, and I wasn't telling them where my money was going on a questionnaire they sent me to fill out. I was not giving in to the demands of the school, especially since I gave them the idea. Again, because it was a literary review, they had difficulty understanding my ideas about limited commercialization. I needed money, so I came up with another idea that I thought was urgently needed in the Blues community, and for the self-reliance of the culture of Blues, as I explained earlier. I decided to combine Blues, literature, lifestyle, and useful information for musicians, industry people, and fans in one magazine. I called it *The Original Chicago Blues Annual.* Original because you know who tries to claim everything as theirs. I wanted to nail down the magazine's creator, intent, and ownership.

By far, OBCA was the best representation of Blues culture in any print media. The idea was conceived and produced by a Black person who is the Blues. And sadly, that's unique, because Blues musicians are still seeking recognition and certification from white people. I mean grown-ass Black people, whose music is at the very core of modern music, are wanting to be authenticated and approved by whites who have absolutely no connection with

their history, pain, social and economic conditions, except for the fact that they continue benefit from the cruelty of their forebearers.

It's a pity. My thinking is that no culture needs to be concerned about approval, ratings, and certification by those of another culture. That's why in OCBA we had no record and performance reviews by the usual cadre of soulless, vacuous scribblers, like Bill Dahl and others who regularly contribute their feebleminded rambling to certain music publications and newspapers. In fact, there were never reviews, only recognition, praises, and blessings. Most of us want our creative efforts to be appreciated. But when you've been conditioned for centuries to believe that you must clear nearly everything with the whites before it has any value, that is nothing less than self-loathing. Plantation-colonial minded white folks have played that against people of colour and native peoples globally for centuries. My position with OCBA was, and still is, I don't give a fuck what Eurocentrism dictates; not about our music, dress, hairstyles, language, nothing. And everything I've just mentioned has been at some point denounced by them, and then eventually, appropriated and profited from by them.

Can you imagine a Manchurian walking around Rome declaring what has value and what does not? Or a native of the Americas questioning the authenticity and quality of the art of Mali? But the Eurocentric mindset has judgment and classifications for nearly everything. And they are kingmakers, crowning some person that has nothing to do with the Black Blues experience as the new beacon of the Blues, and therefore by extension, attempting to alter the history and ongoing experiences of Africans in the Americas. What arrogance!

What stupidity! *Janis Joplin, Paul Butterfield, Mike Bloomfield, Stevie Ray Vaughan, Gary Moore, Joe Bonamassa, Bonnie Raitt,* and on and on. They cool, but they ain't us! Let me be perfectly clear here. There are Blues people, some who happen to play music; and there are people who play and love the Blues, structurally, poetically, and empathetically, but they are not Blues people. They can never be. If they were, they'd be descendants of those who perished on plantations, in the seas, and in the rivers of Black blood and bones. They'd still be shaken by the thought of violated Black wombs. They'd be still reeling from the loss of children and parents on the auction block. They'd still be trying to rip away three hundred years of Christian whitewashing. They would gag at the memory of lynching and cross burnings. They would look in the mirror and love themselves even though they have been lightened by centuries of rape. They would openly venerate *Malcolm X, Medgar Evers, Maya Angelou, Sterling Brown, Nelson Mandela, Trayvon Martin, Fred Hampton, Ida B. Wells, Mackandal*, and on and on. They would hear in the distance, and in their brains incessantly, Black mothers crying, and Black names ringing. The Blues is history, the present, and the future. I know for sure that some heirs to economic and social hegemony truly love the Blues as music and a distinct culture; but being the Blues, that can never be.

You are right. I think outside of United States, there is much more appreciation for Blues culture than within the United States.
That's true to an extent. Academically for sure, and there are diehard fans of Black culture who are not pretending to be anything that they are not. Some of the greatest platforms for performance and study of Blues

and Jazz are in Europe. Some of the best paydays are nearly anywhere outside of the U.S.

A lot depends on who you are dealing with, and one's ability to deal. Remember, the ideas of exploitation, cultural cleansing, genocide, eugenics, Christian domination, Crusades, harsh punishment for so-called heresy and non-compliance, are deeply rooted in Ancient Roman and Judeo-Christian societies. A great deal of that evil can be attributed to Constantine, the Catholic and Anglican Churches, and the menacing kingdoms of Europe and England.

Do you feel that accomplished what you set out to do in publishing?
Yes. From the first chapbook, *I The Blues*, published in 1987, to the coffee table book, *Great Black Music - The Art Ensemble of Chicago,* published in 1997, I'm pleased. There was never a lot of money to work with, but I managed. I published the works of over a hundred writers, poets, photographers, and artists. I feel fortunate to have had the honor to publish or republish some truly creative and inspiring writers and artists. People like *Gwendolyn Brooks, Jayne Cortez, Amiri Baraka, Henry Miller, Deitra Farr, Pinkie Gordon Lane, Eugene B. Redmond, Henry Dumas, J. P. Donleavy, Hart LeRoy Bibbs, Kalamu Ya Salaam, Quincy Troupe, James Otis Williams, Mike Hennessey, Alejo Carpentier, Luis Rodriguez, David Witter, Floyd Webb, Isio Saba, Julie Parson Nesbit, Joan Hackett, Julio Finn, Preston Jackson, Barbara Barefield, David Whiteis, and scores more. And through interviews, to have the thoughts of E. Parker McDougal, Paul Freeman, Johnny Shines, Alvin Singleton, Pinetop Perkins, Billy Boy Arnold, Junior Wells, Famoudou Don Moye, Lester*

Bowie, Eddie Boyd, and others. LaBosse, this was a vision realized. Of course, in retrospect, one can say I should have done this or that differently, but that's what growth is all about. Everything grows, in one direction or another, and hopefully, I'm growing for the better.

No regrets?
Not really. If anything comes close to a regret, it would be disappointment in the then Chicago Public Schools Superintendent, Ted Kimbrough. He committed to buying copies of *Literati Internazionale* for high school libraries. This cat had me come over to the CPS office on Pershing Road to drop of books and pick up a check. I get there, and some lady, a secretary or administrative assistant, is flipping the pages of *Literati Internazionale*. She tells me that the magazine is unfit for high school students. She points out a poem that has the word fuck in it, and the back cover that featured a nude sculptor by the renown artists, *Preston Jackson*. This woman was a total fucking moron. Yet, she convinced Kimbrough to renege on the purchase. I asked her about all of the nudes in European art. So called classic Greek and Roman sculpture. She said that art was classic, and was accepted at such, whereas Jackson's work was not. What damn fools! Kimbrough and his art assessor. Pictures of some 3000-year naked statues of white people are okay, but the work of a well-respected Black artist is not. A long way to go for some of us.

If I recall correctly, during your publishing period you were also involved in other endeavors, right?
During that period, there was certainly a lot going on. In 1991 *I founded Straight Ahead Productions,* a company specializing in concerts, music production, publishing, advertising sales and graphic design. I moved

from an office that was basically a mailbox to one that was around 3000 square feet at 213 W. Institute Place, in River North. Straight Ahead collaborated with an organization, *Jazz in Sardegna,* to co-produce festivals in 1992 and 1993. I brought in Chicago artists *Jimmy Dawkins, Katherine Davis, Tommy McCracken, Deitra Farr, Shirley King,* and others. Also, artists from Iceland were brought in. *Halldor Bragason*, founder of the fine Icelandic band *Vinir Dora,* brought his band to Sardegna along with the spectacular singer, *Andre Gylfadottir.* Straight Ahead was involved with record production. I signed on with *DIW Records Tokyo*, to produce a series of Blues CDs for the company's *GBW* label. GBW means *Greetings From Blues World*, which is how I greeted my Japanese partners once in a letter. They decided to use that as the name of the label. I produced nine CDs. Given the production budget limitations, I think a couple of them came out rather well, particularly those of *Billy Branch*, and my own.

And more importantly, the artists got paid fair money. Nobody walked away complaining, as they often did with some Chicago labels. And a lot of that complaining was often to me, not up in the face of the persons they were complaining about, which is where it should have been. Anyway, I wanted to give the artists sizable advances, and DIW went along with that. I figured, get the artists as much as possible up front, because it can be a long wait to receive royalties, if ever. Plus, a lot of artists don't have a clue about accounting. Record companies can tell you anything. Show you any kind of bullshit piece of paper with numbers. And some of the Blues people were not equipped to question the numbers in a statement, if there was one. Anyway, out of that series there are recordings of *Kay Reed, Valerie Wellington, Billy Branch, Junior Wells, Burning Chicago*

Blues Machine (which was Koko Taylor's band without Koko), and two by me. There is a live compilation recording that we called *Chicago Blues Night,* which featured *Deitra Farr, Jimmy Conley, Tommy McCracken, Katherine Davis, Willie Kent, Shun Kikuta, and me.* There were also collaborations with my friend Halldor Bragason in Iceland. We brought in *Jimmy Dawkins, Pinetop Perkins, Billy Boy Arnold, Shirley King, and Deitra Farr.* Several recordings were made with *Jimmy Dawkins, Pinetop Perkins,* and *Billy Boy Arnold.* Without a doubt, Halldor and I were key in bringing the Blues to Iceland.

Straight Ahead was rolling. What else were you doing besides running Straight Ahead?
I was gigging quite a bit as well. I had lengthy tours in Poland, Italy, Iceland, and Germany during those years. I had many gigs with Jonas Blues Band, fine people, who are musicians from Roma. True believers. I also served on the *Chicago Blues Festival Advisory Committee* from 1987 until 1995, when I had already left Chicago. And I had my family which was always a priority. All and all, I was stretched pretty thin. I got pneumonia in 1992 just before the Sardegna Festivals. I was still recovering when I had to take on managing that situation with loads of unforeseen circumstances, and unpredictable behavior by certain individuals. My assistant, *Minka Maasdam*, was a great help. Anytime you have a large group on the road, you must be in good shape all around. My brain was fine, but I was still weak from pneumonia, even though the sickness had left my body. But things were going along okay, as a company and individually. But you know, anyway you look it, Straight Ahead was a small player in a business of millions. Survival is the key word.

And in 1993, I toured with the *Art Ensemble of Chicago's Salute to the Chicago Blues Tradition.* This was a month-long tour that included Germany, Scotland, UK, Italy, Switzerland, France, The Netherlands, Slovenia, and Austria. The band consisted of the AEC plus guest artists, *Frank Lacey, Herb Walker, James Carter, Amina Claudine Meyers, and me.* This tour was certainly one of the highlights of my music career. To be in such amazing company saluting *Great Black Music,* incomparable!

It was also during this tour that my dear friend Rose Ingraham, the mother of my son, Kevin, passed away suddenly in Los Angeles. Kevin was working as a roadie with the band at that time.

Anyway, another thing that happened was that *Valerie Wellington* and I decided to form an organization that could serve the needs of Blues artists. *We called it The Chicago Blues Artists Coalition.* The focus of the organization was healthcare, fair wages, education, family support, business counseling, event planning, fundraising, and more. We had nearly thirty musicians come to the first meeting. Now Valerie Wellington, she was young and inexperienced when it came to understanding the nature of the club owner plantation mentality, and generally the nature of business. Chicago club owners claim ownership of the musicians who work regularly in their clubs. At that time there were several. I told Valerie the same thing I'm saying today, keep your business away from anybody that's in business on the Chicago Blues Scene. That means club owners, certain people in City Hall, the record label owners, all of them motherfuckers. For you to coalesce is the last thing they want to see happen. They have been exploiting musicians' lack of literacy, business sense, lack of self-confidence, and fear of reprisals for independent thinking for decades. I told Valerie, but she didn't listen. She didn't understand the nature of the beast. She wanted to have meetings at Rosa's lounge, in the belly of the beast. First meeting, Tony Manguillo, the owner of Rosa's, is telling Valerie how to run things. I challenge him because I know he don't know shit about not-for-profits, or anything else other than running his little club over on Armitage. I also suspected that he was a mole. And I believe the only reason he was there or offered his place for the meeting was so that he could go and report back to the other club owners what was up. It hurts me to say this, one by one, tired ass shuffling Blues artists withdrew their interest in the coalition. Some of the Kingston Mines regular performers said that the owner, Doc Pellegrino had warned them, that if they stayed in the coalition, they'd lose their jobs. Some other club owners told the musicians that they would take care of their needs; they didn't need to belong to any kind of organization. These meetings should have been held privately, and completely away from the people you going to try to negotiate with. I said it then, and I'm saying it now. Keep your business secret in Chicago until the time is right, and only release info through the right channels, not some devious-ass club owner looking out for himself.

That's a shame. That Blues people just were not ready for and lacked the courage to bring about a change.
Exactly. And we had good media coverage. *George Papajohn* at the *Chicago Tribune* did a great story, as did *Ebony Magazine*. But fear is a motherfucker. The cadre

of Blues businesspeople struck fear in the hearts of some of Chicago's Blues people with the same old tactic used to prevent slave revolts: turn us against each other.

I know you wanted to cover some recent history before we close out Book 1. In closing, is there anything you'd like to share?
Yes, two things. I left Chicago and went to Montréal in September of 1994. My wife and I had been separated since September of 1992. She moved with our daughter to North Carolina. I hated to see that, I mean I ruled out North Carolina as a place to live, and that was painful because my daughter was there. I wasn't going to live under no southern yoke, or any other for that matter. I felt that I had made a positive contribution to Black Blues culture in Chicago and beyond. I was fatigued. Also, I deeply felt that nothing in the social and economic order of Chicago could ever change. That made my decision to live elsewhere easy. I spent nearly two years in Montréal, then moved to Italy. The first six months were spent nearly in total seclusion in Tuscany. I rented a small two-bedroom house with a frog pond, and lots of land, in a verdant valley near the village of Boccheggiano, which is situated between *Massa Maritima,* and *Siena.* For weeks at a time the only people I spoke with were Adamo, the gardener; the shopkeepers in the village; and Tito Capaccioni the postman, who turned out to be a Blues loving fantastic guitarist. Tito lived in *Massa Marittima,* and organized music festivals. We have been friends since those days. My Tuscany evenings were consumed with reading, writing, music, and listening to the nightly gnarling and grunting of roaming packs of *chingali.*
My father died in November of 1996. I went to see him

in Chicago about two weeks before his passing and stayed another two weeks afterwards looking after his affairs along with my sister. Going through the effects of a person who had a fifty plus years law practice, was all consuming, and overwhelmingly interesting. There was even a good laugh that happened. We found hidden among his old files a magazine called, *Chunky Asses.*

Chunky Asses!
Yeah, the same one that can be seen in the Eddie Murphy movie, 'The Golden Child', in the newsstand scene. I cracked up when I saw this. I mean I'm definitely a booty man, and so was my Dad. I guess it's in the genes. Thank you, Daddy!

Shortly after my return to Italy, I was compelled to end my seclusion for economic reasons. I moved to Rome. We'll get into that intriguing, learning, mostly pleasurable, and sometimes wild part of my life in the coming book. While living in Italy, I married for the fourth time. My wife, Dooney, and her two sons, Luca and Raffy, and I moved to Loulé, Portugal, in the Algarve in April 2001. Another adventure in existing ensued. In 2003, Dooney gave birth to our daughter, Beguine. In January 2005, we relocated to LaGrange Park, Illinois. For the next few years, I maintained a low profile in the Chicago area, but was quite active in Europe. Nothing had changed in Chicago. In fact, from a Blues musicians business perspective, things had gotten worse.
In 2011, I came up with the idea for an ultra-high-tech, interactive Blues museum for Chicago. I found partners, and we cofounded the *Chicago Blues Experience.* Keep your eye on the newspapers.

LaBosse, my friend and brother, thanks for working with me the past three years to bring my memoirs to these pages.

Beau, thanks for the honor. Let's uncork some Champagne. Praises and Blessings.

Praises and Blessings. May the Ancestors be Honored. Ashé

To be continued.

Continuing after excerpt.

I think that excerpt pretty much explains your music and publishing activities, and it also provided a good picture as to your process of becoming who you are.
Yes, it does, and I am continuing with new adventures in publishing. As you know in 2020, I published a multi arts book called Spandana, which means response in Telugu, and motivation in Hindi. The second issue will come out around the same time as this book.

Spandana, The Debut, certainly covered a lot of territory, from poet, Hart LeRoy Bibbs, to the music of the Romani people. You had stunning images from Icelandic photographer *Ásta Magnúsdóttir;* and incredible Detroit Jazz Images captured through the lenses of *Barbara Barefield,* and more and more. Congratulations!
Thank you, LaBosse.

Yes. Springing out of the flashback are continuing parts of the story. As I mentioned my father passed away in

1996 while I was living in Tuscany. When I returned to Italy, for economic reasons I had to move to Rome, and I had fulfilled the purpose of my hermit period which was to regroup spiritually. And now for another example of the Cosmics guiding light.

When I went to Chicago to see my dad, the Alitalia flight was completely booked, only one seat available. I was last to board and was seated in Business Class next to an Alitalia executive, Mona, a beautiful and conversational lady that was headed to Minneapolis. As we got acquainted, I learned that she wrote about travel, and was also a poet. Well, we certainly had similar interest. I told her what I had been doing, including moving to Tuscany. As we continued speaking and having wine and snacks, and becoming more familiar, she talked about an acquittance of hers who worked in the Italian tourism industry, who was once assigned to Chicago, a man by the name of Paolo Ricci. She said that he was great writer, poet, and artist, and that when I returned from Chicago, I should definitely get in touch him. Mona requested paper, pen and envelope from the air host and wrote a short letter of introduction to Paolo. This kind of amenity was the norm on Alitalia Business Class flights. She wrote his phone number on the back of one of her business cards.

That was a nice gesture, to write a letter introducing you. I prefer this way of introduction rather than a text message or email.
Indeed. One gives a call to the person that they are to be introduced to, then explains how they came to be known by the person who wrote the letter that you wish to present. Then a meeting is arranged, the letter is presented and read, and then perhaps some type of rela-

tionship ensues, or not.

That's all done quite swiftly these days with text messages, and emails. The personal touch is missing or dwindling quickly. So, we are moving towards an impersonal society where chance meetings are becoming more and more rare. People are glued to phones and headsets.
Exactly. But a handwritten letter on the author's letterhead within an artistically crafted envelope becomes a memento, a souvenir, that depending on who is involved, may one day be sold at an estate sale years later. But a screen shot of a text message, 'Al, meet Rita; Rita meet Al. You both like Crypto so hey! Go for it!' best, Jessie. The only positive thing from this example is that those in the communication may make some money, then they can pay to go to finishing school.

Ha-ha! Do finishing schools still exist?
I would think so, but unfortunately, and unfairly in my opinion, traditionally these schools were meant for young ladies who were being prepared to step into high society and hopefully land a prosperous husband. Recently, I heard about a finishing school for men in the UK that teaches basic manners, dining etiquette, voice control, *savoir faire*, and a lot more.

This could help bring about a reformation of some blokes who primarily eat fast food, and gobble it down whilst driving, or watching sports on TV with buddies in a man cave along with liters of beer.
That's a hilarious vision, but that's how it be for many.

How long before you and Paolo met?
It was actually quite a while. I returned from Chicago in

early December. I decided to move to Rome in March, but it wasn't a simple move. I had to find a suitable place to live and that took some time. I stayed with a good friend, Daniele Bombasaro at his villa in Ronciglione for a few weeks. Then a friend, Kass Thomas, told me about a recent vacancy in a building her partner's family owned in Monte Sacro not far from Via Nomentana, on Via Carlo Lorenzini. It was perfect. In May I got in touch with Paolo. He invited me to come and visit him and his family at their house in Castiglione Fiorentino, Tuscany.

Was Paolo's place near where you used to live in Tuscany?
No, I lived closer to the sea and the towns of Grosseto and Follonica, Paolo's house was further east between Cortona and Arezzo near the train line to Florence. So, Paolo sent his partner, Dooney, a very attractive and friendly Irish lady, to pick me up at the train station. It was a short ride to their house which typified Tuscan architecture throughout the region. The house was located beyond a front gate surrounded by tress, grass, and flora. The interior had been remodeled and was quite spacious with a massive combined cucina and dining area, and several bedrooms. Paolo and Dooney had twins sons, Luca, and Rafael, who were five years old at that time. This was May of 1997.

How did Paolo respond to the letter from Mona?
He laughed quite a bit and said that he was aware that she had written it as they were in touch often. He also felt that *Letters of Introduction* were once a dignified practice that have fallen by the wayside.
How did you get along with them and did you find some common ground with him having lived in

Chicago?
Actually, I thought his life, and as I found out, their life, as Dooney was there with him, would have connected more with Chicago's unique culture of music, theatre, ethnic neighborhoods, and more, but they had not experienced much in the time that they were there. I thought that was unusual for a poet and visual artist to be in such a land of contrast, cityscapes, and a diverse population to have experienced so little. And when Paolo said that the only Black person that he knew in Chicago was the doorman at the luxury high-rise where they resided, I realized that he was an insular and pompous individual that Mona probably had no real idea about. Still, I was pleased about the introduction, as I needed to make as many contacts as possible, and Dooney seemed like a good person.

That is rather odd behavior for a creative person. Did you keep in touch with them?
I saw them at a dinner on another occasion, and after that we didn't socialize any more, but we had that occasional check-in by telephone.

Now, you're living in Rome, what's going on?
Well, for music things started off slow, then suddenly picked up. I started working a lot on the road. I brought in musicians from Chicago and London to tour with me. I called one tour Chicago Beau, the *SaBoom Boom Gypsy Tour.* We toured extensively around Europe and played many festivals including *JazzWoche Burghausen,* and *April Jazz in Espoo Finland.* That band was *Enrico Liparini, guitar; David Clarke, bass; Thomas Harris, drums; Herb Walker, guitar; and myself.* Another band was *Chicago Beau and his Wonderful Time Band,* with some of the same musicians, and also *Frank Rou-*

leau, drums; Winston Delandro, guitar; and Michael Bailey, bass.

My collaborations with *Jonas Blues Band and Harold Bradley* were always exciting with the band being well studied in the culture and dynamics of the Blues. Over the years we have worked from Rome, to Sardegna, to Sicily, and every place in between. We were on the Gianni Mena Show in Milano, and too many others to remember. And *Harold Bradley,* who was also a former Cleveland Browns football player, brought crooning elegance to the band's performances. At that time band members were, *Luca Casagrande, guitar; Ranieri de Luca, drums; Marco Corteggiani, harmonica; and Gianni Franchi, bass.*

I worked with Italian musician, Alex Britti for many gigs as a band, and as an acoustic duo. We had a lot of fun and brought joy to our fans all over Italy. Alex got a record deal and made several hits for the Italian market, which was very good for him, because he was, and may still be, a person who doesn't like to fly. I haven't spoken with him since he was suddenly propelled into domestic prominence in the late nineties, but he is a vibrant force in the fabric Italian popular culture. Bravo!

Excellent painter and harmonical player, *Gavino Perretta,* and I did a number of gigs including one at a Basilica in Naples where the audience became totally sanctified by my preaching the Blues. The great soul singer, *Herbie Goins, of Herbie Goins & The Night Timers,* owned a club just outside Roma where I did a few gigs. I did guess appearances in Sardegna, and many other gigs there that were arranged by promotor and photographer, Isio Saba, who sadly passed away in 2013. There were some really busy periods, not always, but when things were rolling it was fun and profitable.

There were quite a few Art Ensemble of Chicago gigs where I appeared as special guest including the Art Ensemble of Africa Tour. From Rome I went everywhere doing all kinds of work. Here, I must compliment *GKP Promotions & Mike Hennessey, Isio Saba, Daniel Bombasaro, and Ilse Weinmann* for their cooperation in keeping my bands and me busy through the years.

How was your social life during this period?
It was happening! I had many dinner parties and was invited to many. *Gavino Perretta* is a great cook, as are many Italians, and he prepared marvelous meals. And I had many lady friends that I admired greatly. Oh, I missed a red flag or two in some of those affairs, but time eventually helps one sort things out. I had, and still have a truly amazing circle of friends in Italy from many walks of life including artists, lawyers, designers, musicians, architects, and on and on. And so overall my social life was not lacking in any way.

Would you say living in Italy was fulfilling?
Yes, it was in many ways. Actually, Italy as a country, offered many possibilities, especially to an outsider that were conducive to creativity, and periods of introspective solace. Even though Italy is highly charged politically, I didn't get involved in the national political scene. Sometimes, a political organization would hire musicians at a rally or festival, like the absolutely amazing *Festa de l'Unita*, but that would be the extent of my role. However, global human rights issues, racism, gender equality, child exploitation, that struggle continues

everywhere, and I'm contributing efforts to help that wherever I am.

Italy is a beautiful country with the sea on three sides as well as islands. Ancient history all around, and archaeologists are still uncovering remnants of bygone days. There is much beauty in the past, as well as much destruction, cruelty, greed, and all that lends to the human condition. In Italy there are grim reminders that time will change everything including great empires. In a time-flash, nothing but ruins.

Did you work on other projects when you were performing.
Yes, I did. Lester Bowie of the Art Ensemble approached me about putting together a hardback book about the group, I enthusiastically accepted. Doing this project meant putting in lots of hours and days organizing the different aspects of the book. I needed to travel to Paris, where the group had once lived and made numerous recordings, and I needed to travel to Chicago, where the group had their offices. I had to interview people associated with the group. I had to interview the AEC members. With the help of Famoudou Don Moye, I had to sort through photographs, documents, and memorabilia. After gathering all that I needed, I had to put it all together. Here's where the *Cosmics* show themselves and let you know that they are there for you. I had two good friends who were partners, Sara, and Felix. Sara is graphic designer, and Felix runs a high-end print shop. And they were my neighbors across the hall from me where I lived in Rome. Sara was the design editor, and Felix printed the book, which turned out beautifully and is pictured in these pages. The name of the book is *Art Ensemble of Chicago, Great Black*

Music – Ancient to the Future.

Of course, I have a copy, which has become a collector's item. It's impossible to find it on the websites that sell books, and when it is available, the price is well into the hundreds of dollars. I know the AEC book was one of many projects, gigs, adventures, and social activities that kept you occupied, what else was going on?

Roma is the kind of city that people like to visit. I had visits from many friends and relatives. My cousin Becky from Sacramento visited. My daughter, Jessica, came in from Toronto for a lengthy visit. She and I toured Tuscany and the Amalfi coast together. Some Chicago friends from the Club Damen era visited. The four-level building where I lived in Chicago was in the 1100 block of North Damen Avenue, just south of Division street. I occupied the first floor, and the lower-level apartment, and some wild friends occupied the second and third floor which was one apartment. The building was rocking with dinner parties, music rehearsals, dancing, and various degrees of decadence, hence Erin and Carrie, two of my neighbours and good friends, came up with the name, Club Damen, for the building. And so, several people from that group visited me, and yes, it took me a few days to recover from their madness.

I remember the Club Damen people from when I came to visit you during the Chicago Blues Festival. I think maybe in 1993. I was staying downtown at the Palmer House, and you brought a few people from Club Damen for brunch. And also on that occasion, there were Icelanders that you knew who were also staying in the Palmer House.

Yes, the Icelanders were there, along with me, backing

up *Pinetop Perkins* at the *Chicago Blues Festival*. They were the Blue Ice Band that consisted of *Halldór Bragason, Guðmundur Pétursson, Ásgeir Óskarsson,* and *Haroldyr Porsteinsson,* also great friends, *Júlia Sveínsdóttir* and *Andrea Gylfadóttir* were there. And also, my dear friend, *Linda Carter*, was in town from Toronto. Great times!

Back to Roma.
Ah yes! For a period of about three months, I re-entered the world of investments by helping a friend in London with his commodity futures portfolio. During that period, I commuted back and forth between Roma and London. In London I lived in St. Johns Wood above a pub called the *New Inn on Allisten Road* , which is now a restaurant and a boutique hotel. Every morning I would head down to Cannon Street where my office was via taxi or tube. It was an interesting time, I was able to reconnect with old friends like actor, *Clarke Peters,* who I hadn't seen since the Paris years. One of the great things that happened because of reconnecting with Clarke is that he took me to hear is brother, David, an outstanding bass player, play at a pub in London one night. As a result, David played numerous gigs as the bass player in my band; and it was there that I met the great Blues drummer, Sam Kelly, and that was the beginning of a beautiful friendship and music relationship that continues to grow. There were some fine people in London that I had not seen for quite a while including some from the *Tramp* nightclub scene, including art collector, *Garech de Brún* and his wife, *Princess Harshad Purna Devi of Morvi*. Also, author *Raynes Minns* and her wonderful family in Hampstead had a few spontaneous gatherings of local artists. All in all, my time in London was quite well-spent between work and socializing.

You were certainly busy. Were you still keeping physically fit?
Roma is a walking city, but for sure there are many, many cars, and parking is its own insanity. I did lots of walking, I mean many kilometers in a day. I played tennis a few times, and I also liked to watch tennis. I remember the 1998 Italian Open, I went to root for the Williams sisters, but neither won a title. Venus was defeated by Martina Hingis in the finals, and Serena was eliminated in an earlier round. I did get to speak with Venus Williams who gave me an autograph on the sports section of *Corriere della Sera.*

I know there are always ups and downs, but overall, it seems that your move to Italy was a wise, and beneficial move. Were you confronted by much racism in Italy?

The short answer is no, not much. Generally speaking, because of my profession, there's a lot of interaction on an intellectual and cultural level. I'm not saying that there is not racism in the arts, it just manifests itself differently. Some things that come out of peoples' mouths is based purely on lack of information combined with ignorance. Now, outside of those circles in day-to-day life, I experienced the usual bullshit, like some dumb-ass waiter in the first-class train restaurant wanting to check my train ticket to see if I belonged there. And once in a bank the teller insisted that my American express Travelers Checks were stolen, and that my ID was false, all because he was a racist stronzo, and I told him so. Then once I was playing with a band in Milano, and we had Black female background singers. I was in one hotel, and the singers were staying in another. After the gig I invited everybody to my suite for drinks and relaxation. The hotel manager would not let the Black women come up to my suite, he claimed they were prostitutes, in fact in that ignorant motherfuckers pea brain, all Black women were hookers. The argument became pretty intense, and thankfully, my friend Mark stepped in speaking perfect Italian, calmed the old fool down, and me. So, those kinds of things happened, but that shit happens everywhere, as we know. Could be at a coffee shop in Manhattan.

Yea, that's pretty normal BS that people of colour have to deal with in many places. But as you said, your profession has a lot to do with your surroundings. As we know there has been a flood of Black immigrants to Italy, some treated well, some not so much. And now there are many Black people being born in Italy who are challenging the *status quo* with some success. And there are many who were born there who are still in that gray zone of being citizens, and are still being ostracized. Some Blacks are gaining recognition and contributing positively to the fabric of Italian society, that's great for those who want to address issues with the visibility of public life, and hopefully, their efforts well contribute to the open-mindedness, and quality of life for all Italians.

I think good lessons for Italians to learn are about the events that took place in New Orleans, Louisiana on March 14, 1891. A mob of nearly 20,000 white people lynched 11 Italians in one of the largest mass lynchings in American History. All of the perpetrators were acquitted. Postcards were made of the lynching of Italians, just like Black people, and sent throughout the country.

Also, Columbus day was created to 'whiten' Americans perceptions of Italians, while further isolating and denigrating southern Italians including Sicilians, and Sardinians. On March 21, 1891, Theodore Roosevelt referred to certain people as Dagos, a denigrating name for Italians, and was quite supportive of the lynchings. Of course, many Americans were horrified at what had become nearly the 'norm' in the way Italians, Blacks, and people of colour were being terrorized, hunted, and lynched and the United States. In East Texas, where my father was from and fled, there were constant random killings of Blacks, Mexicans, and anybody else of colour. On July 29, 1910, what is known as the Slocum Massacre took place when whites-initiated genocide by killing as many Black people as they could find during a twenty-four-hour period. Survivors spoke of the horror and passed the stories of white violence and hatred to their descendants, as did members of my family. It is estimated that between 1882 and 1951, around 5,000 people were tortured, hanged, burned alive, dragged behind trucks; and in some cases, their bodies were dismembered with body parts being kept for souvenirs.

I'm glad we spoke about racism in Italy and the US, and of course elsewhere. I think it's important to be able to see things as they are. There are so many conflicts within all cultures, and when a person realizes that this world is about bitter truths, it can only be stupidity or pure evil that keeps them in a *state of denial*, like so many are.

Moving on, Beau, what else was happening?
I like those words, 'state of denial.'

Anyway, I decided in February of 1999 to make a grand

swoop to Chicago to visit some friends and family, then to North Carolina to see my daughter, and then on to Rio de Janeiro to celebrate my fiftieth birthday. I was completely ready to go wild when I came down with an awful case of the Flu. So, unfortunately, I spent three days in bed at the *Sheraton Grande*. On the fourth day I felt well enough to party and have some fine poolside dining experiences with friends *Gigi* and *Bibiana,* from Natal, who had arranged my trip to Rio. By the fifth day I was feeling much better and that timed perfectly with our Carnival plans where Gigi had purchased *VIP camarotes*.

Ah! I know Gigi from many past adventures! How many were you?
We were six, Gigi, Bibiana, Isabella, Ligia, Rafaela and me. And we had a blast: drinking, laughing, and enjoying the floats, dancers, and all of the aspects of the parade. There have been so many films and documentaries made about the Carnival that I'm not going into details, but basically, it's well organized, and most of what we see in those presentations is how it is. Afterwards, we all went back to the Sheraton for more drinks and late night eats. Ligia, Isabella, and Rafaela, were my guests for the evening. *Esplêndida!*

I think Brazil is an experience one should have, and that means spending lots of time travelling the country and getting to know the people and the many cultures that make Brazil the country that it is. I didn't have time to do that, but I certainly expect to at some point in the future. Of course, under the current president, I would say keep as far away as possible. Brazilian friends have told me that the sadness from Covid deaths never stops, and that their narcissistic president is absolutely impervious to the massive human suffering in his country.

It seems that he has a particular dislike for the indigenous population, and the poor.
That is what many Brazilians are saying and feeling. And of course, since narcissist have no empathy, some can fake it, or try to reverse the perception, but who they really are eventually comes out. Hopefully, Brazilians will rebound soon!

How long was your excursion or swoop as you call it from Roma?
I was gone about a month. When I got back, I got it was back to the business of music. I hooked up with *Enrico Lipparini* and we did a tour in France that included Limoges, Avignon, Lyon, and other cities. And things just kept on rolling.

I know 1999 was a very busy year, and not all fun and work. I remember our conversation when you were in Pomigliano d'Arco, when you said Lester Bowie was ill with hepatitis, and possibly cancer.
Yes, that's correct. In August of 1999, I went to Brooklyn to interview Lester, trumpet player and co-founder of the Art Ensemble of Chicago, for his biography. By that time Lester had been diagnosed with terminal liver cancer, unfortunately, we were never able to finish the project; however, the interview we did about his time in Nigeria with *Fela Anikulapo-Kuti,* is available in my multi arts book, *Spandana, The Debut Issue.*

Lester passed into *Ancestorhood* on November 8, 1999. I returned to New York for his services along with Sardinian promoter, *Isio Saba*, a good friend of Lester's who was very influential in getting Lester and the AEC established in Italy. The Art Ensemble has done several tributes to Lester, as well as other members that have entered the Ancestor Realm, *Joseph Jarman*, and *Malachi Favors Maghostut.*

The world celebrated the beginning of a new millennium with the arrival of the year 2000. What was happening with you?
2000 was the first year that I brought my band to *April Jazz* in Espoo, Finland as part of my *SaBoom Boom Gypsy Tour.* I had wonderful players in that band: *Thomas Harris,* great friend, and collaborator from Montréal, on drums. I had *Herb Walker* from Chicago as musical director, and on guitar. Also on guitar was the *'Pride of Limoges,' Enrico Lipparini,* also known as 'Little Henry.' On bass was *Dave 'Ba-Boom-Ba-Bam' Clark* from London.

Beau, if you don't mind, let's digress briefly so that you can explain to our readers about the *SaBoom Boom Gypsies.*
Absolutely. I gave the tour that name as a tribute to my ancestors and their survival as runaway slaves. There were three main escape routes used by runaway slaves. Some went north to free states like Pennsylvania and New York. Others made it to Nova Scotia, and other parts of Canada. And some, like my father's relatives in Texas, made it to Mexico. There were many fife and drum bands that roamed around the southern states, many escaped slaves had music talents as they were often used to entertain their slave-masters, and also their guests at parties, etc. Some roving bands of escaped slaves were called *SaBoom Boom Gypsies* because they could be heard approaching playing

drums, usually a big bass drum that went Boom! Boom! And others were playing trumpets, fiddles, hand-made instruments and more, while singing and dancing. The children would shout, *Here come the SaBoom Boom Gypsies / Aqui vienen los gitanos de Saboom Boom.* The SaBoom Boom Gypsies not only played music, but some were also story tellers, quite like the *Griots* in African tradition. I heard these stories from my father, and his older brother, Dell, who spent a lot of time in Mexico before and after The Great War. In 1922 my father went to Merida and found many of our relatives. Some had married Mexican Black people who were from families freed from slavery in Mexico. Also, I have an uncle who married into a Romani family, who are called *Gitanos.*

And so, The SaBoom Boom Gypsy Tour was honoring runaway slaves everywhere as well as my relatives. As part of the tour, we sometimes walked onto the stage playing African drums, and shouting the names of Ancestors. We did several such tributes honoring Lester Bowie.

Generally speaking, Romani people do not like to be called Gypsies, as the word has derogatory implications for many who use it, for others there is a kind of romantic fantasizing about a nomadic lifestyle that has nothing to do with their culture. For my family, and many others, there was no connection with what would come to be the racist and cruel treatment of Romani across Europe and elsewhere. We were called SaBoom Boom Gypsies, and there was no disrespect. And personally, I feel a deep kinship with the Romani because of shared history in Mexico and other places, and our struggle to maintain and nurture our own identities.

Beautiful explanation. Viva los Gitanos SaBoom

Boom! Back to April Jazz!
April Jazz is one of the great festivals in Europe, not too big, so a kind of intimacy is possible between the artists and the audience. That was the beginning of an eleven-year relationship with that Festival. I became the emcee, and also gave lectures at the local high school. I got to know some really fine people including artists coordinator, *Susanna Torvinen*. During those years I had the opportunity to connect with artists that I greatly admire like *Pharoah Sanders, Bo Diddley, Simone, Richard Bona, Al Jarreau, George Duke* who I reconnected with, and so many others. And there were great Jam Sessions at the Tapiola Garden Hotel, as that's where most of the artists were staying. Unfortunately, *Marrti Lappalainen,* who founded the festival and the Espoo Big Band, passed away in 2012. That resulted in the festival's new administration and artistic director initiating changes that reflected their thinking, and not Martti's so much, therefore changes were made that did not include my participation. But that was a beautiful run, but all things change with time.

Didn't you do a film with the Espoo Big Band and drummer, *Billy Cobham?*
Yes, that was certainly one of the highlights of my work in Finland. The film is called *Sonic Mirror*, and it's a documentary made in 2007 about *Billy Cobham,* and directed by *Mika Kaurismäki*. It follows his music journey in various parts of the world including Brazil, Switzerland , and Finland. There's a section with the *Espoo Big Band* that's shot live, and I am the *Master of Ceremony.* I suggest our readers visit the IMDb website to learn more and find out where to see the film.

And what more in 2000?

At some point I got back in touch with Dooney in Tuscany. Her life had changed considerably, as she was no longer with Paolo, they had split up. She was living in a lovely country house with her two sons in *Camucia*, a town near *Cortona*. And so, over a few months, of visiting back and forth, and lengthy discussions about possibilities as a family, we decided to spend more and more time together. Of course, that meant that we each had to dissolve whatever affairs in which we were involved. During that period Dooney met my son *Kevin*, and daughter, *Jessica*. She also met *Carrie*, one of the wild and crazy women from *Club Damen*.

Dooney was learning about my past, family, and friends, a good thing. And she introduced me to her friends, and I met her mother who visited from Germany.

Also, during this period, my friend and Blues singer, Deitra Farr and her son, Daniel, moved to Rome from Chicago. Deitra stayed at my place while she got her life in Italy organized that included finding a school for her son, and eventually an apartment for them. Since I was spending more and more time with Dooney, Deitra had my place to herself much of the time.

Eventually, my landlord asked me to move so that his mother could move in. Fact is, the apartment was purchased for her anyway, but she never wanted to live there, that's why it was available to me. Things change. In one short period, Deitra moved out, and I moved to Camucia with Dooney. All good.

How was your new life in Tuscany, revisited?
Ha-ha! It was drastically different than my hermit period in *Boccheggiano*. As you know, Tuscany has some famous towns that have reputations for various reasons.

Pisa, Florence, Grossetto, Siena, and others have some kind of attraction. It could be sheer beauty, art and architecture, incredible wines, or parties and nightlife. *Cortona,* which sits on a hill is known for stunning architecture, vistas, restaurants, and the activity and beauty of *Piazza della Repubblica.* Dooney knew quite a few people, good people, so our *Cortona* evenings were filled with dining and café socializing, as her children played with other children in the Piazza. Everything seemed quite wholesome, but as we know, in small towns there is usually some drama taking place. In Cortona it was mostly harmless hearsay and gossip about some people's sexual romping that was the catalyst for shocked faces, raised eyebrows, and whispering.

How long were you living in Tuscany before moving on?
About six months. And things were pretty good, even though work had slowed down a bit. I had a few good gigs. One was back in the states at the *University of Maryland,* where I did a lecture and Blues concert at the *Nyumburu Cultural Center.* I had not been there since the center's founder, James Otis Williams passed away in 1998. That was a great gig arranged by Otis's successor, *Dr. Ronald Ziegler,* and it was also a tribute to Otis.

Dooney accompanied me on gigs in *Palermo* and *Bari,* and that was nice to get to know each other better. It was in *Palermo* that I introduced her to the Blues Cocktail Lounge Aphrodisiac from the Southside of Chicago!

Man, you crazy! Every neighborhood has their own mythical 'get naked potion,' what was yours?

Quite simple. Three shots of *Grande Fine Champagne Cognac,* five shots of *Coca-Cola*, and one ice cube. Works every time. Look out, *Sildenafil!*

Please continue.
Dooney and I decided to get married. I thought Iceland would be a good place because I could arrange a few gigs there at the same time, thereby paying for our stay, and travel. The plan worked, and we were married in Reykjavik Town Hall on January 22, 2001, which is also my daughter Jessica's birthday. A few friends attended the ceremony including *Andrea Gylfadottir, Kristen Mary Swenson,* who was Dooney's Maid of Honor, and *'Gumi' Guðmundur Pétursson,* who was my Best Man. Later that evening I played a gig with *Gumi* and his band that was televised nationally, then we went on tour for two weeks. Dooney returned to Italy the day after our wedding, and when I returned, a new chapter commenced.

A new chapter indeed. What happened next?
Dooney introduced the idea of possibly moving to the Algarve in Portugal. Her dad, Noel, had left a beautiful property to his children, Verena, Dooney, Leona, and Alba. The property had two houses, a larger main house that was over 100 years old, and a smaller house that was once a stable, that had recent converted into an excellent living space. Also, there's an orange and lemon grove that have nearly a hundred trees. The larger house was soon to be vacated by Noel's wife, Catharine, as she had built a new home nearby from the ground up. This presented an opportunity for us to move there. There was some family discussion between Dooney and her sisters, and it was finally agreed that we would move in. And so, in April of 2001 we

moved to Loulé, Portugal.

The Algarve certainly has a different pace than Italy. In fact, the pace is rather slow. What were your first impressions, early experiences?
The first people I met were friends of Dooney's family, and some Portuguese people who worked for them. Some of them had been in the Algarve for years and had lovely homes and thriving businesses. Some just lounged about and enjoyed their wealth. Most of them treated the Portuguese as inferior. They were mostly English, arrogant, and blatantly racist, and that included Catharine O., who liked to throw the 'N' word around, even in public places. And the only reason I put up with her ignorant ass is that I didn't want to spend time in a Portuguese jail. However, another issue arose one day within the family that questioned her honesty and integrity, as a result I had the pleasure of putting her out of the house, escorting her to the front door whilst denouncing her as the wretched hag she is. She had been penalized. A few of the haughty types around possessed low-life characteristics that I have vast experience dealing with. Generally, I avoided them, because I wasn't going to let them try to provoke me into perhaps, kicking they ass. That wasn't going to happen.

You know LaBosse, as a Black man observing the condescending attitude of certain Brits towards the Portuguese, I found it rather amusing. At one point these two, among others, were competitors in colonizing and the slave trade. They both invoked a brutal hypocrisy: Bible in hand, slave shackles in the other, with rape, gold, land, and your soul, their priority.

But the motherfuckers could not get our souls. We continue to survive through our resilience and *Ancestor Brilliance!* No doubt the British were the biggest winners of the greed war, with the Portuguese lagging far behind. The resentment can be felt throughout the Algarve where the English are thoroughly entrenched, with some putting on airs with the intent of irritating their Portuguese hosts. I know the Portuguese never imagined themselves to be in the role of gardeners, laborers, butlers, nannies, and other domestic help for the English. Maybe one day, as a result of a cosmic anomaly, everything will suddenly be reversed or dramatically altered. That would be amusing to watch from the sidelines!

Now, that I've gotten the arrogant assholes out of the way. In Portugal I met some wonderful people with wide souls who enjoyed life and were from all over the place. I came to know musicians, bankers, teachers, doctors, and tennis partners. I played a gig here and there, but there were not any Blues bands or Blues festivals in the area. There was an annual Jazz Festival in Loulé, and Rock Festivals in many of the coastal towns.

But the country is alive with its own music like *Fado, Pimba,* the music of *Cape Verde, Portuguese Jazz,* and a lot more. And the country has many concerts and festivals in its different regions. I had the honor of performing at a Jazz Festival in *Cascais* near Lisbon, with the great Portuguese singer, *Maria Viana.* And by the way, Maria is one of the organizers of the *Cascais Jazz Club.*

Were you busy outside of Portugal?
Oh yes! I was back and forth to Finland. I also did a tour in Spain with drummer, *Frank Rouleau, guitarist, Winston Delandro,* and bassist, *Michael Bailey.* I did a week

at the *Half Note* in Athens along with drummer, *Sam Kelly,* from the UK, and Icelandic guitarist, *'Gumi' Guðmundur Pétursson.* And that gig was special in many ways because I got to see some old friends from my younger days in Greece including *Pierretta Lorentzatou,* who is now among the Cosmics.

But you know, after the September 11 attack on the World Trade Center, things seemed to slow down a bit. And after George Bush ordered the absolutely senseless attack on Iraq, which wasn't based on anything but his menacing ego, his impulsiveness, and his need to kill, even people that had nothing to do with the attack on the WTC and had no WMDs as he and his lackeys claimed, things really slowed. There were cancellations in several places including Istanbul, Paris, Rome, and Hanover

How did you manage with work drying up?
It was tough at times, as we were a family of four, soon to be five. My daughter, Beguine, was born July 29, 2003. Then in November I became ill and was in Faro Hospital for nearly a month.

Muito obrigado ao excelente Sistema de Saúde de Portugal pelo atendimento que me dispensou quando estive extremamente doente. Você é o melhor!

Many thanks to the excellent Health Care System in Portugal for the care given to me when I was extremely sick. You are the best!
I recovered and did a gig in Chicago in 2004. During the summer of 2004 I organized gigs for myself and several other musicians at different venues around the Algarve, that project was fairly lucrative. But as you

said, there is no pace in the Algarve, no hustle. It's impossible to hit the streets in a resort area and find people interested in doing something. Most of them are settled and set in their ways.

It became increasingly clear that changes had to be made soon. Not only were gigs drying up, but the political climate was worsening daily internationally, and some arts organizations that I had been doing business with said that their funding was also drying up because of uncertainties.

What steps did you take to resolve matters?
Dooney and I talked about solutions. And even though I dreaded the idea, I thought going to North America may create some opportunities. I looked at possibilities, and spoke with many contacts in Montréal, Toronto, San Francisco, and Los Angeles. Chicago was the choice mainly because of my history there. And we didn't want to raise the kids in LA, which was only considered because of the climate. Montréal was a consideration, but that involved many immigration formalities that would take a lot of time.

In November of 2004, I went to Chicago. The family came on January 17, 2005. We lived in LaGrange Park, Brookfield, and Oak Park. For the most part I maintained a low profile in Chicago, but continued to work occasionally in Finland, Germany, and Canada.

I've been working a lot in Montréal and other parts of Québec with my old friend, *Jean-François Fabiano,* who is also a fantastic drummer, composer, and songwriter. We've done a lot together including recordings, and we have big plans for the future. His wife, *Anne-Marie*

Meunier, manages the bands bookings, and she does an absolutely fantastic job. In Chicago in 2010, *I published a compilation of the Original Chicago Blues Annual titled BluesSpeak,* that was published by the *University of Illinois Press.* That helped to gain some traction.

As I mentioned near the end of *Too Much Unconvenience,* I had an idea for a Blues Museum for the City of Chicago, *The Chicago Blues Experience.* I presented the idea to several people, and eventually I found people who were interested in the project. The team committed to trying to make it happen at a meeting on December 18, 2011. That's ten years ago. No, it has not opened, and the *Chicago Blues Experience* team is no more. The *core* team of *original co-founders* put in years of hard work and commitment for which I am greatly appreciative.

Beau, your closing thoughts, advice.
This has always been an insane world with soulless, upright-walking creatures, similar in appearance to normal empathetic human beings, in control of much that goes on in the world. I see many people withdrawing from the institutional hypocrisy that has caused unspeakable misery to indigenous people and others across the planet for centuries solely for greed, ownership, and the feeding of the narcissistic cravings of political, royal, and religious hierarchy. I say, continue the withdrawal!

To my Blues Sisters and Brothers, I say,
OWN IT! IT'S OURS!

Praise onto the Cosmics, Ancestors, Orishas, and Loa!

Copyright 2021, Lincoln T. Beauchamp, Jr.

www.chicagobeau.net

www.LTBeauchampPublishing.com

www.Spandana.net

www.ingramcontent.com/pod-product-compliance
Lightning Source LLC
Chambersburg PA
CBHW071921290426
44110CB00013B/1440